BR
WAR
& A
ES

HMS Tireless

THE ROYAL NAVY

It is now over a year since the Strategic Defence and Security Review, published in October 2010, set out the road map for the future defence and security of the United Kingdom. Such were the scale of the cuts, with wholesale capabilities withdrawn and a "scorched earth policy" of scrapping or destroying the hardware associated with those capabilities, being implemented with such haste, that, even today, the SDSR remains a topic of heated debate within defence circles.

Since the previous edition of this book, the Royal Navy has witnessed the decommissioning of the last four Type 22 frigates, bringing an end over thirty years of Type 22 operations - and significantly the RNs at-sea intelligence collection capabilities. Also consigned to the scrapheap has been the RN carrier strike capability and the RAFs Maritime Patrol asset, the Nimrod.

All of these cuts were sold to the public as a necessary reshaping of our Armed Forces after the Cold War, essential to make them more relevant and more flexible and expeditionary in nature - better able to react to the unpredictable nature of the threats that we, as a nation, are likely to face in the future. Those in the know, of course, saw through this propaganda and recognised the SDSR for what it really was - a cost cutting exercise driven by the need to save money, rather than by a strategic need to defend our nation. It was obvious that it was not going to take much to put our already overstretched forces under considerable strain.

The government has justified the cuts, and the withdrawal of what would seem to be essential capabilities for an island nation - Maritime Patrol and delivery of a strike capability from the sea - by stating that the gaps created could be mitigated by the deployment of other assets. In the case of Maritime Patrol, the Type 23 frigates, MCMVs, Merlin helicopters and C-130 Hercules transport aircraft would step into the breach and provide both coastal and offshore security in addition to protection of our continuous at sea deterrent force as the submarines transit to and from their patrol areas from their Clyde base.

Carrier strike however remains in limbo while our new Queen Elizabeth class aircraft carriers are built - with a little luck, and a lot of investment, the UK could have a credible at sea strike capability by the middle of the next decade.

However, within months, the SDSR had been proved to be severely flawed and ill-conceived.

North Africa, it would seem, had not been privy to the aims of the SDSR, and in early 2011 a wave of public uprisings swept through North African countries as their citizens sought to secure a better future, a democratic future, for themselves. Much of this "Arab Spring" was relatively peaceful, with a change in leadership being brought about following mass public protest. However, not all regimes were prepared to give in easily. Egypt eventually forced regime change, which in turn seemed to encourage other nations to rise up - however, their leaders were less inclined to relinquish the reins of power. Yemen, Libya and Syria were determined to suppress the uprisings and the latter two regimes turned on their citizens with the full might of the police and military.

Initially, the World nations deployed assets to the Mediterranean to ensure the safety of their own people. The UK was in the fortunate position to have the Response Force Task Group - a newly formed Amphibious Group - operating in the area. Some of the ships were redeployed at short notice and sailed into Libyan ports to evacuate non-Libyan nationals. The RN was able to evacuate personnel to Malta - the irony being that the ships being used were scheduled to be scrapped on their return to the UK as surplus to requirements.

After the civilian population of Libya began to suffer brutal suppression at the hands of the Libyan regime it was inevitable that some sort of intervention would be required. The USA were not keen to get involved in yet another Arab conflict, arguing that North Africa was on Europes doorstep and therefore a problem more suited to Europe to sort out.

The UK Prime Minister led calls for a no-fly zone to be imposed and pressed the UN and Europe for such action. He seemed to forget that he had recently initiated a round of swingeing defence cuts which had reduced UK assets to the bone. He also seemed to forget that UK troops were already heavily committed to military operations in Afghanistan. By May, the United Nations and Europe had declared a no-fly zone and deployed aircraft to Mediterranean airbases from where they could strike at Libyan targets. The Royal Navy was key to these initial strikes having deployed the submarine TRIUMPH which was able to strike targets ashore with her Tomahawk cruise missiles. She was temporarily relived by TURBULENT as she returned to the UK to reload before returning to the Mediterranean for further strike operations.

The majority of the strike effort was from the air. One of the key tasks before the strike aircraft could begin operations was to conduct intelligence collection over the target areas. Again there was a single aircraft available - the Nimrod R1. The government was forced to extend the aircraft in service for an additional few months to enable it to conduct this vital role, before it to was released from duty and returned to the UK to be taken out of service. Specialist aircraft were required to map movements of ground targets and personnel to enable accurate strike packages to be formed. This required Sentinel aircraft to be redeployed from Afghanistan in order to be available for this key role. On completion of their Afghanistan mission this is yet another aircraft which is going to be withdrawn from service.

In addition to the submarine operations, the RN was initially deployed off shore to provide embargo operations, but as the conflict ashore moved along the coast, the destroyer LIVERPOOL was able to provide naval gunfire support (yes, she too will decommission this year!). Much has been said about the lack of RN carrier strike during this operation. ARK ROYAL with a squadron of Harriers onboard would have been a very useful asset - having ground attack aircraft based close offshore and able to react at short notice to emerging threats is without doubt nice to have. However, the truth of the matter is that there were other carrier strike assets in the area (French and Italian, together with a US Navy LHD and her Harriers) and more importantly, the UK Harrier Force had been so poorly underfunded, particularly with regards to operations at sea, that at the time of decommissioning of the ARK ROYAL and her aircraft, there were only eight carrier qualified pilots, only one of which was night certified.

The RN however, did come into its own when it was realised that helicopters were required to operate "low and slow" to be able to identify friendly and enemy targets in the built up areas as the fighting moved into the cities. OCEAN was on hand to host initially four and finally five Army Apache attack helicopters. Providing this attack capability offshore is exactly what carrier strike is supposed to do - something we as a nation will not now be able to do in any strength for maybe more than a decade. The Libyan crisis has probably done the RNs case for carrier strike no end of good!

By September, the crisis in Libya was all but over and assets were slowly returning home. But, this small intervention has highlighted the flaws in the SDSR. Although only operating a limited air campaign with very little opposition, the UK found itself in far from ideal circumstances. Air strike operations were launched from various land bases in the Mediterranean where we had to negotiate basing rights - in fact had the operation run on much beyond September some of the aircraft would have to have been moved from their operating bases a at the request of the host nation as their presence was disrupting commercial operations at the bases. Our lack of certain capabilities were only mitigated by having a coalition of NATO nations, some of whom were able and willing to step into the breach.

However, it was the lack of an at sea strike capability which really stood out. Less than six months after decommissioning the nation's remaining carrier strike assets, planners had to rely on long transit flights and all of the associated in flight refuelling required to maintain a strike cycle, while the French, Italians and US Navy were able to launch effective strike packages from carriers and LHDs stationed in the central Mediterranean. It can only be hoped that the government were stung by this embarrasing failure and will now put their full weight behind the Queen Elizabeth class carriers, which are still by no means out of the woods with regard to cancellation or curtailment of the project.

The Libyan crisis also highlighted the sheer lunacy of the governments assertion that it could mitigate the loss of Maritime Patrol through the use of other assets. Although a relatively minor campaign, Libya proved that the UK could, in even the smallest of crises, no longer provide security around her own coast. As a consequence of needing ships to operate in the Central Mediterranean, there was a period in October when the RN could not provide a single frigate/destroyer as a Fleet Ready Escort (FRE) - the ship on standby in UK waters to respond to any emergent threat or crisis, be it a natural disaster at sea, counter terrorism, foreign incursion - or protection of the Trident submarines. The assertion that a frigate, MCMV, Hercules or Merlin would be on hand is pure fantasy - all of these assets are fully stretched conducting their routine day-to-day tasking. I have yet to see any evidence of a Merlin being deployed to Scotland for MPA or Deterrent escort duties.

The RN top brass have contended that the minimum number of destroyers/frigates needed to maintain current commitments was 32. Those commitments remain - indeed with the need to provide assets for counter-piracy operations it could be argued that they have increased, yet the number of frigates/destroyers has been slashed to just 19, not all of which can be operational. With the spectre of possible intervention in Syria, maybe even further action in the Gulf region, it can only be a matter of time before the deck of cards comes tumbling down.

Having also written a 1952 version of *British Warships & Auxiliaries* recently to commemorate the Diamond Jubilee of Her Majesty the Queen, it was inevitable that I would compare the two editions - and in both instances the RN finds itself in a very similar situation.

In both 1952 and 2012 the UK is crippled with debt in the midst of a recession. The Armed Forces are undergoing a period of transformation as they seek to reshape themselves for the future. The RN in 1952 was facing large scale obsolescence in the wake of technological advances at the end of World War II and needing to adapt to the challenges of a Communist Russia which was beginning to field a growing modern submarine fleet. Both in 1952 and 2012, the government was faced with decreasing income, but increasing demands for equipment. However, today, the response is to cut assets and capabilities in the name of transformation while in 1952, the government embarked on a massive programme of re-equipment and modernisation to meet the emerging threat from Communist Russia.

But why the different approaches. Why is the government of today not seeing the need for a strong capable RN equipped with sufficient destroyers and frigates to ensure the security of our maritime borders. Why is the government of today not providing work to our shipyards and aircraft industry by ordering much needed equipment to boost both our defences and our economy by creating a manufacturing base, thus ensuring employment and renewed economic growth? Why is it that modern government can only see the armed forces as a drain on resources and a prime candidate for clawing back money for spending on vote winning departments such as Health and Social Security?

The answer is that in 1952, the country had just emerged from all out war - most, if not all, of the government would have experienced war first hand; would have seen the UK being blitzed; soldiers and civilians being killed in huge numbers. That concentrates the mind. In 1952 the government were in the job of defending the UK against such further aggression - they were prepared to pay what it took to ensure that UK Plc could defend itself when needed.

Today, I suspect that not a single politician in cabinet has witnessed all out war, probably never even come under fire. For them they have lived through a generation of relative peace - despite the fact that our soldiers, sailors and airmen remain engaged in combat operations in Afghanistan. Our government have become complacent. They no longer see the need to pay for a comprehensive national insurance policy for our island nation. Temporary capability gaps become the norm and after a while are consigned to history. If you pay reduced premiums don't be surprised that when you have to claim, you get a lot less than you imagine. This nation, and its Armed Forces, deserve better than third party, fire and theft funding.

Steve Bush
Plymouth 2011

6

SHIPS OF THE ROYAL NAVY
Pennant Numbers

Ship	Pennant Number	Page	Ship	Pennant Number	Page
Helicopter Carriers			NORTHUMBERLAND	F238	21
			RICHMOND	F239	21
ILLUSTRIOUS	R06	13			
			Submarines		
Assault Ships					
			VANGUARD	S28	9
OCEAN	L12	14	VICTORIOUS	S29	9
ALBION	L14	15	VIGILANT	S30	9
BULWARK	L15	15	VENGEANCE	S31	9
			TURBULENT	S87	12
Destroyers			TIRELESS	S88	12
			TORBAY	S90	12
DARING	D32	16	TRENCHANT	S91	12
DAUNTLESS	D33	16	TALENT	S92	12
DIAMOND	D34	16	TRIUMPH	S93	12
DRAGON	D35	16	ASTUTE	S119	10
DEFENDER	D36	16			
DUNCAN	D37	16	**Minehunters**		
LIVERPOOL	D92	18			
EDINBURGH	D97	19	LEDBURY	M30	22
YORK	D98	19	CATTISTOCK	M31	22
			BROCKLESBY	M33	22
Frigates			MIDDLETON	M34	22
			CHIDDINGFOLD	M37	22
KENT	F78	20	ATHERSTONE	M38	22
PORTLAND	F79	20	HURWORTH	M39	22
SUTHERLAND	F81	20	QUORN	M41	22
SOMERSET	F82	20	PENZANCE	M106	24
ST ALBANS	F83	20	PEMBROKE	M107	24
LANCASTER	F229	20	GRIMSBY	M108	24
ARGYLL	F231	20	BANGOR	M109	24
IRON DUKE	F234	20	RAMSEY	M110	24
MONMOUTH	F235	20	BLYTH	M111	24
MONTROSE	F236	20	SHOREHAM	M112	24
WESTMINSTER	F237	21			

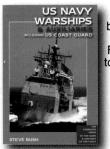

HMS Vengeance

SUBMARINES
VANGUARD CLASS

Ship	Pennant Number	Completion Date	Builder
VANGUARD	S28	1992	VSEL
VICTORIOUS	S29	1994	VSEL
VIGILANT	S30	1997	VSEL
VENGEANCE	S31	1999	VSEL

Displacement 15,980 tons (dived) **Dimensions** 149.9m x 12.8m x 12m **Speed** 25 + dived **Armament** 16 Tubes for Trident 2 (D5) missiles, 4 Torpedo Tubes **Complement** 135

Notes

After the first successful UK D5 missile firing in May '94 the first operational patrol was carried out in early '95 and a patrol has been constantly maintained ever since. The UK's Trident missiles have been de-targeted since 1994, and the submarine on deterrent patrol is normally at several days notice to fire her missiles. VIGILANT, the third vessel to enter the refit cycle, arrived at Devonport on 11 October 2008 and was refloated in June 2011. She is due to sail for sea trials this year. In 2010 the Government revealed plans to extend the service life of the Vanguard class to beyond 2028 while at the same time reducing the number of operational missiles on each submarine to just eight. To achieve the five year extension will require three additional Long Overhaul Periods (LOPs), at Devonport, costing around £1.3 billion between 2014 and 2024.

HMS Astute

ASTUTE CLASS

Ship	Pennant Number	Completion Date	Builder
ASTUTE	S119	2009	BAE Submarine Solutions
AMBUSH	S120	Building	BAE Submarine Solutions
ARTFUL	S121	Building	BAE Submarine Solutions
AUDACIOUS	S122	Building	BAE Submarine Solutions
ANSON	S123	Planned	BAE Submarine Solutions
AGAMEMNON	S124	Building	BAE Submarine Solutions
AJAX	S125	Planned	BAE Submarine Solutions

Displacement 7,400 tonnes (7,800 dived) **Dimensions** 97m x 11.2m x 9.5m **Speed** 29+ dived **Armament** 6 Torpedo Tubes; Spearfish torpedoes; Tomahawk cruise missiles **Complement** 98 (Accommodation for 12 Officers and 97 Ratings)

Notes

Significantly larger than previous RN SSNs the Astute class is designed to fulfil a range of key strategic and tactical roles including anti-ship and anti-submarine operations, surveillance and intelligence gathering and support for land forces. Ordered in 1997, the Astute class were intended, initially, to replace the S class in RN service. The initial history of the programme was one of severe overspend and delays, leading in 2003 to a restructuring of the entire contract.

The first of class ASTUTE was delivered in 2009 and commissioned on 27 August 2010. AMBUSH was launched (rolled out from Devonshire Hall) on 16 December 2010 and conducted her initial basin dive in October 2011. The keel for AUDACIOUS was laid on 24 May 2009 and for the fifth boat, ANSON, on 13 October 2011. The go-ahead has been given to start the procurement process of long lead items for AGAMEMNON with first steel due to be cut this year.

ASTUTE, achieved its in-service date in April 2010 and is currently undertaking a period of extensive and comprehensive sea trials before being handed over to the Royal Navy for operational service, which on current plans will be in late 2012. In November 2011 she successfully fired her first Tomahawk missiles during trials off the USA, where she will operate until the Spring before returning to the UK for her first operational deployment.

The planned in-service dates for the remainder of the Astute class boats are: AMBUSH (2013); ARTFUL (2015); AUDACIOUS (2018); ANSON (2020); AGAMEMNON (2022) and AJAX (2024).

HMS Triumph

TRAFALGAR CLASS

Ship	Pennant Number	Completion Date	Builder
TURBULENT	S87	1984	Vickers
TIRELESS	S88	1985	Vickers
TORBAY	S90	1986	Vickers
TRENCHANT	S91	1989	Vickers
TALENT	S92	1990	Vickers
TRIUMPH	S93	1991	Vickers

Displacement 4,500 tons 5,200 tons dived **Dimensions** 85.4m x 9.8m x 9.5m **Speed** 30+ dived **Armament** 5 Torpedo Tubes; Spearfish torpedoes; Tomahawk cruise missiles **Complement** 130

Notes

TORBAY, TALENT, TRENCHANT and TRIUMPH have undergone upgrade and received Type 2076 Sonar. Tomahawk Cruise Missiles are fitted in TRIUMPH, TURBULENT, TORBAY and TRENCHANT. It is expected Tomahawk will eventually be fitted in all of these boats. TRIUMPH and TURBULENT were deployed off Libya in 2011 and it is known that TRIUMPH fired several Tomahawk missiles during the conflict. TURBULENT is scheduled to decommission this year. Other decommissioning dates are TIRELESS (2013); TORBAY (2015); TRENCHANT (2017); TALENT (2019) and TRIUMPH (2022).

HMS Illustrious

LANDING PLATFORM HELICOPTER (LPH)

INVINCIBLE CLASS

Ship	Pennant Number	Completion Date	Builder
ILLUSTRIOUS	R06	1982	Swan Hunter

Displacement 22,500 tonnes **Dimensions** 210m x 36m x 6.5m **Speed** 28 knots
Armament 2 - 20mm guns, 3 Goalkeeper **Aircraft** Tailored Air Group (Merlin, Sea King, Chinook, Apache as required) **Complement** 726 + 384 Air Group (600 troops)

Notes

With the withdrawal of the Harrier from service in April 2010 she now operates in the LPH role. She emerged from refit at Rosyth in July 2011. In October and November 2011 the ship underwent a seven week period of operational sea training to prepare her for her new role before taking over from OCEAN in early 2012. As part of the 2010 SDSR announcement it was revealed that both ILLUSTRIOUS and OCEAN would be the subject of a short study to determine which vessel best fulfills the LPH role - the result being that ILLUSTRIOUS is scheduled to serve in the LPH role until OCEAN completes her refit around 2014. At that time ILLUSTRIOUS will be withdrawn from service.

HMS Ocean

OCEAN

Ship	Pennant Number	Completion Date	Builder
OCEAN	L12	1998	Kvaerner

Displacement 22,500 tonnes **Dimensions** 203.8m x 35m x 6.6m **Speed** 17 knots **Armament** 3 x Phalanx, 4 x 20mm BMARC guns, 4 x Minigun **Aircraft** Tailored Air Group (Merlin, Sea King, Chinook, Apache as required) **Complement** Ship 285, Squadrons 206 (maximum 1275 including Royal Marines)

Notes

Can carry 12 Sea King and 6 Lynx helicopters. Frequently employed as the flagship of the UK Amphibious Ready Group. RAF Chinook helicopters are normally carried as an integral part of the ship's air group, but they are unable to be stowed below decks. Modified with two 50m blisters attached to the hull at the waterline below the after chine to improve safety margins while deploying LCVPs from the after davits. Vessel is somewhat constrained by her slow speed. Many improvements have been made to her including accomodation for both crew and embarked Royal Marines; advanced communications facilities; a better weapon defence system and an upgrade to the ship's aviation support facilities to improve support to helicopter operations including the Apache attack helicopter, which she embarked in 2011 for operations off Libya. She will now undergo a major refit, prior to returning to service in 2014.

HMS Bulwark

LANDING PLATFORM DOCK (LPD)

ALBION CLASS

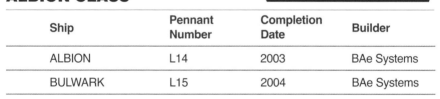

Ship	Pennant Number	Completion Date	Builder
ALBION	L14	2003	BAe Systems
BULWARK	L15	2004	BAe Systems

Displacement 18,500 tons, 21,500 tons (flooded) **Dimensions** 176m x 25.6m x 7.1m
Speed 18 knots **Armament** 2 x CIWS, 2 x 20mm guns (single) **Complement** 325
Military Lift 303 troops, with an overload capacity of a further 405

Notes

Vehicle deck capacity for up to six Challenger 2 tanks or around 30 armoured all-terrain
tracked vehicles. Floodable well dock able to take four utility landing craft. Four smaller
landing craft carried on davits. Two-spot flight deck able to take medium support helicopters
and stow a third. BULWARK emerged from a refit in 2011 which saw her flightdeck recon-
figured to allow the simultaneous operation of two Chinook helicopters. These vessels do
not have a hangar but have equipment needed to support aircraft operations. Only one of
the class will remain operational at a time. BULWARK assumed the role of fleet flagship in
October 2011. ALBION has entered a period of extended readiness after which she will
undergo a regeneration refit and rejoin the fleet in 2016.

DESTROYERS
DARING CLASS
(Type 45)

Ship	Pennant Number	Completion Date	Builder
DARING	D32	2008	BVT Surface Fleet
DAUNTLESS	D33	2008	BVT Surface Fleet
DIAMOND	D34	2009	BVT Surface Fleet
DRAGON	D35	2011	BVT Surface Fleet
DEFENDER	D36	2012	BVT Surface Fleet
DUNCAN	*D37*	*Building*	*BVT Surface Fleet*

Displacement 7,350 tons **Dimensions** 152.4m x 21.2m x 5.7m **Speed** 29 knots **Armament** 1 - 4.5-inch gun, Sea Viper missile system comprising Sylver VLS with combination of up to 48 Aster 15 and Aster 30 missiles **Aircraft** Lynx or Merlin **Complement** 190 (with space for 235)

Notes

Originally to have been a class of up to 12 ships this was reduced to just six. The bow sections, funnels and masts were built at Portsmouth and then transported by barge to Govan where final assembly and fitting out takes place. DARING was commissioned on 23 July 2009 and declared operational on 31 July 2010. DAUNTLESS was handed over to the RN in December 2009 and DIAMOND on 22 September 2010. The fourth vessel

DRAGON was handed over in August 2011, with DEFENDER commencing her stage 1 sea trials in October 2011. She is scheduled to commence stage 2 trials early this year with handover planned for the latter half of the year. The final vessel, DUNCAN, was launched on 11 October 2010 and is expected to go to sea this year. In September 2009 a £309m contract was awarded to BVT Surface Fleet for the in-service support for the Type 45 class for up to seven years, starting in January 2010.

DRAGON is the first of the batch two destroyers, which include upgrades to systems onboard in line with technological developments.

In September 2010 DAUNTLESS successfully conducted the first High Seas Firing of the Sea Viper anti-air guided weapon system, the first time that the missile had been fired from a Type 45 destroyer. DARING successfully proved the system in May with her first high-seas firing.

This year has been dubbed the year of the Type 45, by the MoD, as the first vessels prepare for their maiden operational deployments. DARING completed her operational sea training at the end of 2011 and has been fitted with her pre-deployment upgrades, including two Phalanx CIWS mountings. DARING, DAUNTLESS and DIAMOND are all scheduled to deploy, though at the time of going to press precise deployment details had not been released.

HMS Liverpool

SHEFFIELD CLASS
(Type 42) Batch 2

Ship	Pennant Number	Completion Date	Builder
LIVERPOOL	D92	1982	C. Laird

Displacement 4,820 tonnes **Dimensions** 125m x 14.3m x 7m **Speed** 29 knots **Armament** 1 - 4.5-inch gun, 4 - 20mm guns, Sea Dart Missile System: 2 - Phalanx, Lynx Helicopter **Complement** 287

Notes

In 2009 LIVERPOOL underwent a £6 million, 10-month refit at Portsmouth. The work package included the fitting of a transom flap for greater fuel efficiency; upgrades to the ship's weapons and sensors and installation of WECDIS, the electronic chart and navigation system. She has also had a full refurbishment of her Aft Auxiliary Machine Room, taking receipt of 2 new Reverse Osmosis plants as well as the replacement or refurbishment of a number of her generators and main propulsion engines. She deployed in 2011 as part of the Response Force Task Group (RFTG), but was soon diverted to operations off Libya in support of the United Nations and NATO where she remained until October 2011. The last of the Batch 2 Type 42s she will decommission this year after 30-years of service.

18

HMS Edinburgh

SHEFFIELD CLASS
(Type 42) Batch 3

Ship	Pennant Number	Completion Date	Builder
EDINBURGH	D97	1985	C. Laird
YORK	D98	1984	Swan Hunter

Displacement 5,200 tonnes **Dimensions** 141m x 15.2m x 7m **Speed** 30 knots + **Armament** 1- 4.5-inch gun, 2 - Phalanx, 2 - 20mm guns, Sea Dart missile system, Lynx Helicopter **Complement** 287

Notes

Stretched versions of earlier ships of this class. Designed to provide area defence of a task force. Deck edge stiffening fitted to counter increased hull stress. Both are fitted with the 4.5-inch Mod 1 gun. YORK fitted with Phalanx Block 1B. Vessels are now frequently seen without the distinctive radome covers over their Type 909 trackers. Despite the announcement that there will now only be six Type 45 destroyers built, the intention is to decommission all of the Type 42 destroyers before the final Type 45 enters service. MANCHESTER & GLOUCESTER decommissioned in 2011, YORK will decommission this year and EDINBURGH in 2013.

HMS Westminster

FRIGATES
DUKE CLASS (Type 23)

Ship	Pennant Number	Completion Date	Builder
KENT	F78	2000	Yarrow
PORTLAND	F79	2000	Yarrow
SUTHERLAND*	F81	1997	Yarrow
SOMERSET*	F82	1996	Yarrow
ST ALBANS	F83	2001	Yarrow
LANCASTER*	F229	1991	Yarrow
ARGYLL*	F231	1991	Yarrow
IRON DUKE*	F234	1992	Yarrow
MONMOUTH*	F235	1993	Yarrow
MONTROSE*	F236	1993	Yarrow

Ship	Pennant Number	Completion Date	Builder
WESTMINSTER*	F237	1993	Swan Hunter
NORTHUMBERLAND*	F238	1994	Swan Hunter
RICHMOND*	F239	1994	Swan Hunter

Displacement 4,900 tonnes **Dimensions** 133m x 16.1m x 5m **Speed** 28 knots **Armament** Harpoon & Seawolf missile systems: 1 - 4.5-inch gun, 2 - single 30mm guns, 4 - 2 twin, magazine launched, Torpedo Tubes, Lynx or Merlin helicopter **Complement** 185

Notes

Now the sole class of frigate in RN service, the ships incorporate 'Stealth' technology to minimise magnetic, radar, acoustic and infra-red signatures. Gas turbine and diesel electric propulsion. Those ships marked * have been fitted with the Mk 8 Mod 1 4.5-inch gun. Type 2087 Sonar is to be fitted in only 9 of the remaining 13 of the class (ARGYLL, MONTROSE, MONMOUTH and IRON DUKE will not receive the upgrade). In 2010 WESTMINSTER emerged from refit at Devonport as the first of class to receive both the Seawolf missile system upgrade and the new DNA(2) command system. ARGYLL returned to service in 2010 following an 11-month refit at Rosyth, the first Type 23 to undergo a second major refit.

In August 2008 the MoD announced that the Type 996 surveillance and target indication radar is to be replaced by the ARTISAN 3D Medium Range Radar (now designated Type 997) under a £100 million contract covering demonstration, manufacturing, delivery and the first 10 years of in-service support. The ARTISAN 3D (Advanced Radar Target Indication Situational Awareness and Navigation) is a modular open architecture maritime radar system designed to deal with complex littoral environments. It is planned to be incrementally installed between 2011 and 2015. IRON DUKE will receive its new radar during a refit period scheduled to start this year.

The Seawolf missile system is expected to reach the end of its service life around 2018 and studies are underway for a replacement system. The MoD and MBDA have been involved in preliminary studies to define and develop a common solution for such anti-air target guided weapons, used for naval, land and aerial operations which could be implemented in a future system currently known as CAMM – the Common Anti-air Modular Missile, to be fielded in 2015-2018. The CAMM family is being designed to meet the MoD's requirement for a Future Local Area Air Defence System (FLAADS) for the Type 23 Frigate and, subsequently, for the Future Surface Combatant.

Under current plans ships are scheduled to decommission as follows: ARGYLL 2023; LANCASTER 2024; IRON DUKE 2025; MONMOUTH 2026; MONTROSE 2027; WESTMINSTER 2028; NORTHUMBERLAND 2029 ; RICHMOND 2030; SOMERSET 2031; SUTHERLAND 2033; KENT 2034; PORTLAND 2035 and ST. ALBANS 2036.

HMS Ledbury

MINE COUNTERMEASURES SHIPS (MCMV)
HUNT CLASS

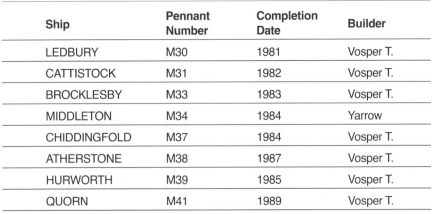

Ship	Pennant Number	Completion Date	Builder
LEDBURY	M30	1981	Vosper T.
CATTISTOCK	M31	1982	Vosper T.
BROCKLESBY	M33	1983	Vosper T.
MIDDLETON	M34	1984	Yarrow
CHIDDINGFOLD	M37	1984	Vosper T.
ATHERSTONE	M38	1987	Vosper T.
HURWORTH	M39	1985	Vosper T.
QUORN	M41	1989	Vosper T.

Displacement 750 tonnes **Dimensions** 60m x 10.5m x 3.4m **Speed** 15 knots **Armament** 1 x 30mm + 2 x Miniguns **Complement** 45

Notes

The largest warships ever built of glass reinforced plastic. Their cost (£35m each) has dictated the size of the class. Very sophisticated ships - and lively seaboats! All are based at Portsmouth as the Second Mine Countermeasures Squadron (MCM2).

BAE Systems has been awarded a six-year contract worth £15m to replace the propulsion systems on these ships, with the work to be carried out at Portsmouth. The first new propulsion system was expected to be installed on board CHIDDINGFOLD in late 2011, with upgrades to the remaining seven ships taking place during planned ship docking periods up to 2016. The re-propulsion project will involve the installation of new engines, gearboxes, bow thruster systems, propellers and machinery control systems.

LEDBURY to decommission in 2019, CATTISTOCK, BROCKLESBY, CHIDDINGFOLD and MIDDLETON 2020, HURWORTH and ATHERSTONE 2022 and QUORN 2023. In order to keep up the overseas deployment tempo, crews can be swapped between ships. MIDDLETON and QUORN are forward deployed to the Gulf.

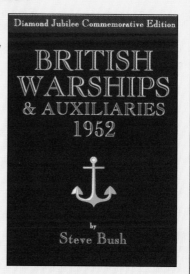

HMS Shoreham

SANDOWN CLASS

Ship	Pennant Number	Completion Date	Builder
PENZANCE	M106	1998	Vosper T.
PEMBROKE	M107	1998	Vosper T.
GRIMSBY	M108	1999	Vosper T.
BANGOR	M109	2000	Vosper T.
RAMSEY	M110	2000	Vosper T.
BLYTH	M111	2001	Vosper T.
SHOREHAM	M112	2001	Vosper T.

Displacement 600 tons **Dimensions** 52.5m x 109.m x 2m **Speed** 13 knots **Armament** 1 - 30mm gun; 2 x Miniguns; 3 x GPMG **Complement** 34

Notes

A class dedicated to a single mine hunting role. Propulsion is by vectored thrust and bow thrusters. All are based at Faslane as the First Mine Countermeasures Squadron (MCM1). The ships are manned by eight numbered crews which are rotated throughout the fleet allowing deployed vessels to remain on station for extended periods. RAMSEY and PEMBROKE are forward deployed to the Gulf. WALNEY decommissioned at Faslane on 15 October 2010 as a defence economy and is for sale at Portsmouth.

HMS Tyne

PATROL VESSELS
RIVER CLASS

Ship	Pennant Number	Completion Date	Builder
TYNE	P281	2002	Vosper T.
SEVERN	P282	2003	Vosper T.
MERSEY	P283	2003	Vosper T.

Displacement 1,677 tonnes **Dimensions** 79.5m x 13.6m x 3.8m **Speed** 20+ knots
Armament 1 x 20mm; 2 x GPMG **Complement** 48

Notes

Ordered on 8 May 2001, the deal was unusual in that the ships were leased from Vospers (VT) for five years under a £60 million contract. Thereafter the opportunity existed for the lease to be extended, the ships purchased outright or returned to VT. So far the arrangement seems to have been a success with VT meeting their commitment of having the ships available for over 300 days a year. In January 2007 a £52 million lease-contract extension was awarded extending their RN service to the end of 2013. DEFRA is at an advanced stage in negotiations with the Marine Management Organisation on the continuance of this contract. The River class are now the only RN ships conducting Fishery Protection patrols in the waters around England, Wales and Northern Ireland. The cost to the public purse over each of the last 5 years for operating the three River class was £7.3 million per annum.

HMS Clyde

BATCH II RIVER CLASS

Ship	Pennant Number	Completion Date	Builder
CLYDE	P257	2006	VT Shipbuilding

Displacement 1,847 tonnes **Dimensions** 81.5m x 13.6m x 4.15m **Speed** 19 knots (full load) 21 knots (sprint) **Aircraft** Flight Deck to take Lynx, Sea King or Merlin Helicopter **Armament** 1 - 30mm gun; 5 x GPMG; 2 x Minigun **Complement** 36 (space for additional 20 personnel - see note)

Notes

Designed to carry out patrol duties around the Falkland Islands and their dependencies, the ship is able to accommodate a single helicopter up to Merlin size. She deployed to the Falklands in August 2007. CLYDE's more modern design has enabled her to remain on task in the South Atlantic until later this year. Like the previous River class, she had been leased from BAE Systems, for a period of five years. In July 2011 it was announced that BAE Systems had been awarded a six-year contract extension to deliver support services to the ship until 2018. The annual cost to the public purse of operating the ship is £3.5 million.

CLYDE is able to embark a Military Force of up to 110 personnel (the size of the Roulement Infantry Company (RIC)) and move them around the Falkland Islands, inserting them at will.

HMS Sabre

LIFESPAN PATROL VESSELS (LPVs)

Ship	Pennant Number	Completion Date	Builder
SCIMITAR	P284	1988	Halmatic
SABRE	P285	1988	Halmatic

Displacement 18.5 tons **Dimensions** 16m x 4.7m x 1.4m **Speed** 27+ knots
Armament 2 x GPMG **Complement** 4

Notes

Purpose built in 1988 for counter terrorism duties on Lough Neagh, Northern Ireland. Operated in anonimity until withdrawn from service in 2002, following a review of RN operations in the Province. Transferred to Gibraltar in September 2002 to join the Gibraltar Squadron. On completion of trials they were commissioned on 31 January 2003 and renamed SCIMITAR (ex-GREYFOX) and SABRE (ex-GREYWOLF). Tasked with ensuring the security and integrity of British Gibraltar Territorial Waters (BGTW), the Squadron is permanently assigned to the Operational Command of Commander Joint Operations at Gibraltar.

HMS Raider

COASTAL TRAINING CRAFT
P2000 CLASS

Ship	Pennant Number	Completion Date	Builder
EXPRESS	P163	1988	Vosper T.
EXPLORER	P164	1985	Watercraft
EXAMPLE	P165	1985	Watercraft
EXPLOIT	P167	1988	Vosper T.
ARCHER	P264	1985	Watercraft
BITER	P270	1985	Watercraft
SMITER	P272	1986	Watercraft
PURSUER	P273	1988	Vosper T.
TRACKER	P274	1998	Ailsa Troon
RAIDER	P275	1998	Ailsa Troon
BLAZER	P279	1988	Vosper T.
DASHER	P280	1988	Vosper T.

Ship	Pennant Number	Completion Date	Builder
PUNCHER	P291	1988	Vosper T.
CHARGER	P292	1988	Vosper T.
RANGER	P293	1988	Vosper T.
TRUMPETER	P294	1988	Vosper T.

Displacement 54 tonnes **Dimensions** 20m x 5.8m x 1.9m **Speed** 20 knots **Armament** 1 x GPMG (Faslane based vessels) **Complement** 5 (with accommodation for up to 12 undergraduates).

Notes

Fourteen P2000 craft form the First Patrol Boat Squadron, whose primary role is to support the University Royal Naval Units (URNU) but also contribute to a wide range of Fleet tasking. Commodore Britannia Royal Naval College has overall responsibility for the URNUs whose role is to educate and inform a wide spectrum of high calibre undergraduates. Training is conducted one evening a week in shore units at or near the University and at sea, over the weekends and during the vacations, by a dedicated patrol craft. Vessels are assigned to the following URNUs: ARCHER (Aberdeen); BITER (Manchester); BLAZER (Southampton); CHARGER (Liverpool); TRUMPETER (Bristol); EXAMPLE (Northumbria); EXPLOIT (Birmingham); EXPLORER (Yorkshire); EXPRESS (Wales); PUNCHER (London); RANGER (Sussex); RAIDER (Cambridge); SMITER (Glasgow); TRACKER (Oxford).

The last two vessels built, RAIDER and TRACKER, have a higher top speed of 24 knots as they are fitted with two MTU V12 diesels.

DASHER and PURSUER were transferred to Cyprus at the end of 2002 to form a new Cyprus Squadron to patrol off the Sovereign Base Areas. They returned to the UK in 2010 and now form the Faslane Boat Squadron where they conduct security tasks on the Clyde. They are fitted with ballistic protection around the flying bridge and are armed with General Purpose Machine Guns.

HMS Scott

SURVEY SHIPS
SCOTT CLASS

Ship	Pennant Number	Completion Date	Builder
SCOTT	H 131	1997	Appledore

Displacement 13,300 tonnes **Dimensions** 131.5m x 21.5m x 9m **Speed** 17 knots
Complement 63 (42 embarked at any one time)

Notes

Designed to commercial standards SCOTT provides the RN with a deep bathymetric capability off the continental shelf. Fitted with a modern multi-beam sonar suite she can conduct mapping of the ocean floor worldwide. She carries a mixture of the latest UK and US survey equipment. The sonar system is US supplied. She operates a three watch system whereby the vessel is run by 42 of her ship's company of 63 - with the remainder on leave. Each crew member works 75 days in the ship before having 30 days off, allowing her to spend more than 300 days at sea in a year. Extensive use of commercial lean manning methods including unmanned machinery spaces, fixed fire fighting systems and extensive machinery and safety surveillance technology. Her hull is Ice class 1A: Ships with such structure, engine output and other properties are capable of navigating in difficult ice conditions, but only with the assistance of icebreakers.

• DAVID HANNAFORD   **HMS Enterprise**

ECHO CLASS

Ship	Pennant Number	Completion Date	Builder
ECHO	H 87	2002	Appledore
ENTERPRISE	H 88	2003	Appledore

Displacement 3,500 tonnes **Dimensions** 90.6m x 16.8m x 5.5.m **Speed** 15 knots
Armament 2 x 20mm **Complement** 48 (with accommodation for 81)

Notes

In June 2000, a £130 million order was placed with prime contractor Vosper Thornycroft to build and maintain, over a 25 year period, these two new Survey Vessels Hydrographic Oceanographic (SVHO). Both vessels were built by sub-contractor Appledore Shipbuilding Limited. They have a secondary role as mine countermeasures flag ships. The total ship's company is 72, with 48 personnel onboard at any one time working a cycle of 75 days on, 30 days off, allowing the ships to be operationally available for 330 days a year. Utilizing a diesel electric propulsion system, they have three main generators. They are the first RN ships to be fitted with Azimuth pod thrusters in place of the more normal shaft and propellor. Each ship carries a named survey launch, PATHFINDER (ECHO) and PIONEER (ENTERPRISE). ECHO left Devonport in the first week of 2011 on a two-year deployment to the Red Sea, Arabian Gulf, Indian Ocean, the Middle and Far East.

31

HMS Gleaner

INSHORE SURVEY VESSEL

Ship	Pennant Number	Completion Date	Builder
GLEANER	H86	1983	Emsworth

Displacement 22 tons **Dimensions** 14.8m x 4.7m x 1.6m **Speed** 14 knots **Complement** 8

Notes

Small inshore survey craft used for the collection of data from the shallowest inshore waters. She uses multibeam and sidescan sonar to collect bathymetry and seabed texture data and compile an accurate and detailed picture of the seabed. She was scheduled to decommission in 2007, but she emerged, in 2008, from a Service Life Extension Programme, which will enable her to remain in service for a further 10 years. She carries the prefix Her Majesty's Survey Motor Launch or HMSML.

HMS Protector

ICE PATROL SHIPS
PROTECTOR

Ship	Pennant Number	Completion Date	Builder
PROTECTOR	A173	2001	Havyard Leirvik (Norway)

Displacement 4,985 tons **Dimensions** 89.7m x 18m x 7.25m **Speed** 15 knots
Armament Miniguns; GPMGs **Complement** 88

Notes

The ice-breaker MV POLARBJORN has been leased on a three-year contract from the Norwegian company GC Rieber Shipping as a temporary replacement for the damaged ENDURANCE. Following an intensive 10-day refit at Odense, Denmark, she sailed for Portsmouth where she was commissioned as PROTECTOR on 23 June. The contract for the lease of the ship, worth £26 million over three years, also includes full contractor support and some fitting or refurbishment of equipment for use by the RN. In addition to this, a further £3.7 million has been spent to fit military task equipment such as survey boats and communications equipment. Although the ship has a flight deck, there is no hangar, so she will be unable to deploy with an embarked helicopter. Initially she has been fitted with a pair of Pacific RIBs and a fast rescue craft. She will also deploy with three BV206 all terrain vehicles and three quadbikes and trailers to assist in moving stores and equipment. She will also embark the Survey Motor Boat JAMES CAIRD IV. For future deployments she will embark landing craft for the resupply role. She sailed for her first Antarctic deployment in November 2011.

DAVID WALTER

HMS Endurance

ENDURANCE

Ship	Pennant Number	Completion Date	Builder
ENDURANCE	A171	1990	Ulstein-Hatlo

Displacement 5,129 tons **Dimensions** 91m x 17.9m x 6.5m **Speed** 14.9 knots **Armament** Small arms **Aircraft** 2 Lynx **Complement** 116

Notes

Chartered for only 7 months in late 1991 to replace the older vessel of the same name. Originally M/V POLAR CIRCLE, renamed HMS POLAR CIRCLE (A176) and then purchased by MoD(N) and renamed again in October 1992 to current name. Historically spent 4-6 months each year in the South Atlantic supporting the British Antarctic Survey. Following a flooding incident off Chile in 2008 she was returned to the UK aboard a heavylift ship in April 2009. She has remained at Portsmouth ever since.

It remains unclear whether ENDURANCE will be repaired or disposed of. A long awaited decision on the ship's future is anticipated to be made this year.

Griffon 2400TD

ROYAL MARINE CRAFT

4 GRIFFON 2400TD LCAC

G.R.T. 6.8 tons **Dimensions** 13.4m x 6.8m **Speed** 35 knots **Range** 300 nm
Armament 1 x GPMG **Complement** 2 Crew; 16 fully-equipped marines.

Notes

Ordered in June 2008, these four Landing Craft Air Cushion (Light) (LCAC) have replaced the four 2000TD(M) which were operated by 539 Assault Squadron. The 2400TD offers greater payload, performance and obstacle clearance than the earlier craft, and centre sections of the cabin roof can be removed in order to embark two one-tonne NATO pallets. They can be transported on a standard low loader truck or in the hold of a C-130 Hercules aircraft. They can also operate directly from the well-deck of RN amphibious ships. They are equipped with a 7.62mm General Purpose Machine Gun, HF and VHF radios, radar, GPS, ballistic protection and a variety of specialised equipment. The first hovercaft began sea trials in September 2009 and all four entered service by the end of 2010.

SPECIALIST CRAFT

In addition to the familiar Rigid Raiding Craft and Rigid Inflatable Boats the Royal Marines operate the Offshore Raiding Craft (ORC). It can be configured to transport up to eight fully-equipped commandos at speeds of over 35 knots. It can also be fitted with bullet-proof panels and weapon mountings to become a heavily-armed fire support vessel. Other vessels available include air transportable Fast Insertion Craft (FIC) with a speed of 55 knots in addition to advanced wave piercing designs. Swimmer Delivery Vehicles (SDV), in reality miniature submarines, which can be deployed from dry deck shelters on larger submarines, are also a part of the UK Special Forces inventory.

10 LCU Mk10

Pennants L1001 - L1010 **G.R.T.** 240 tons FL **Dimensions** 29.8m x 7.4m x 1.7m **Speed** 8.5 knots **Complement** 7

Notes

Ro-Ro style landing craft designed to operate from the Albion class LPDs. Ordered in 1998 from Ailsa Troon. The first two were delivered in 1999. The remainder were built by BAE Systems at Govan. Capable of lifting one Main Battle Tank or four lighter vehicles. Capacity for 120 troops. With a range of around 600 nautical miles – more if auxiliary tanks are added – is designed to operate independently for 14 days with its seven man Royal Marine crew in both arctic and tropical climates. All the crew members have bunk accommodation and there is a galley and store rooms. Rather than their pennant numbers, the vessels display alpha-numeric codes signifying their parent ship (A - ALBION; B - BULWARK, P - RM Poole).

The MOD is trialling the PACSCAT (Partial Air Cushion Supported Catamaran), a high-speed landing craft developed by Qinetiq. Between August and December 2010, the craft was put through its paces at Instow in North Devon and in Scottish waters with ALBION. Similar in dimensions to the LCU Mk10 the craft is entirely constructed out of aluminium and is designed to offer the triple benefits of speed, manoeuvrability and payload capacity. It is 30 metres in length, just under eight metres in width and is capable of carrying loads weighing up to 55 tonnes. Propulsion is provided by a pair of MJP water jets powered by MTU-made diesel engines and during trials the craft has demonstrated speeds in excess of 30 knots.

23 LCVP Mk5

Pennants 9473, 9673-9692, 9707, 9708 **G.R.T.** 25 tons FL **Dimensions** 15m x 4m x 1.5m **Speed** 20 knots **Complement** 3.

Notes

First one ordered in 1995 from Vosper Thornycroft and handed over in 1996. A further four were delivered in December 1996 to operate from OCEAN, with two more for training at RM Poole ordered in 1998. A further 16 were ordered from Babcock in 2001. The Mk 5 can lift 8 tonnes of stores or a mix of 2 tonnes and 35 troops. These vessels have a greater range, lift and speed than the Mk4s which they replaced.

In 2011 Sweden lent the UK a pair of rebuilt CBR 90 combat boats for a period of six months of trials to see if they can be loaded and unloaded from UK Amphibious Ships. The vessels have previously operated from the docks of the Albion class but had not been embarked on OCEAN. The boats were converted to enable them to be deployed by davit giving the RN the ability to deploy combat boats in support of operations in the littoral environment. A similar trial is being conducted with the Amphibious Ships of the Dutch Navy. It is not known whether the UK will buy CBR 90s or whether they will join with the Swedish Navy on joint operations.

SHIPS FOR THE FUTURE FLEET

QUEEN ELIZABETH CLASS AIRCRAFT CARRIERS

After a decade of design studies, a contract for the construction of two aircraft carriers, QUEEN ELIZABETH and PRINCE OF WALES, the largest warships to be designed and built in the UK, was signed in July 2008 between the Government and the Aircraft Carrier Alliance, an industrial group comprising BAE Systems Surface Ships, Babcock Marine, Thales and the Ministry of Defence.

The ships are being built in sections constructed by BAE Systems at Govan, Scotstoun and Portsmouth; Babcock in Rosyth and Appledore; Cammell Laird in Birkenhead and A & P, Tyne to be assembled in Number 1 Dock at Rosyth. The dock at Rosyth has had the entrance widened from 124 feet to 138 feet. The sides were re-profiled with the removal of angled steps to make the dock floor 30 feet wider. A new overhead crane with a span of 394 feet, named Goliath, has been installed to straddle the dock and lift the smaller blocks into place. The individual blocks are built under cover and fitted out with machinery and sub-assemblies such as diesel generators, offices, cabins and galleys before they are moved to Rosyth. They have to fit each other precisely and a tolerance of only 10mm is allowed. Work started on the bow section for QUEEN ELIZABETH in December 2008 at Babcock's Appledore Shipyard; lower block 03 weighing about 8,000 tonnes was delivered from Govan to Rosyth in August 2011.

The completed ships will be 932 feet long with a waterline beam of 128 feet and beam across the flight deck of 239 feet. Height from the bottom of the hull to the masthead will be 187 feet and draught 33 feet. There are 9 decks in the hull with another 9 in the islands. Each ship is expected to be in the dock for two years and will be 'floated out' into the adjacent non-tidal basin for completion. The ships were originally intended to operate the F-35B STOVL variant of the Joint Strike Fighter, but the 2010 SDSR decision to operate the conventional F-35C 'tail-hook' variant came too late to modify the first ship. She will, therefore, be completed without the ski-jump and operate helicopters after 'first of class' trials in 2018. The Alliance is working closely with the USN on the electro-magnetic aircraft launch system (EMALS) and advanced arrester gear being developed for the Gerald Ford class and these will be installed in PRINCE OF WALES during build for completion in 2018. She will have two EMALS, each 328 feet (100 metres) long and capable of launching an aircraft weighing up to 99,206lb (45,000 kg) at up to 130 knots end speed every 45 seconds. The decision to fit QUEEN ELIZABETH with catapults and arrester gear at her first refit, once PRINCE OF WALES is operational, has not yet been taken but is likely after the next Defence Review in 2015.

TRIDENT REPLACEMENT PROGRAMME

Initial Gate approval has been given to start design work for the UK's Successor nuclear-powered ballistic missile submarine.

Announcing the start of the programme's Assessment Phase on 18 May 2011, Secretary of State for Defence also confirmed that the next generation SSBN design would be powered by a brand new Pressurised Water Reactor nuclear plant design known as PWR-3. The Successor submarine programme projects the delivery of three or four SSBNs to replace the RN's four existing Vanguard-class submarines from 2028 to maintain continuous at-sea deterrence (CASD).

The decision to push ahead with replacing the Vanguard class submarines was confirmed in the 2010 Strategic Defence and Security Review, although a parallel 'Value for Money Study' specifically addressing the costs of the deterrent programme resulted in a number of changes to the original acquisition plan. For example, the decision was taken to run on the current Vanguard class boats to the late 2020s/early 2030s, re-profile the build schedule for the Successor submarines (with the first now delivered in 2028 rather than 2024), reduce the number of missiles per boat from 12 to eight, and defer a decision on the replacement of the current warhead.

As part of the Coalition Agreement between the Conservative and Liberal Democrat parties, the latter secured a pledge that the government would continue to look for alternatives to the sea-based deterrent. As such, a separate study is under-way to review the associated costs, feasibility and credibility of alternative systems. As recently as 31 October 2011 the Government confirmed their stance on CASD. In response to a question in the House, the Secretary of State for Defence confirmed that, " Continuous at Sea Deterrence (CASD) remains the backbone of our deterrence pos-ture, ensuring a credible and capable deterrent against blackmail and acts of aggres-sion against the UK's vital interests including her NATO allies. CASD is the UK's most enduring current operation and has been successfully delivered for over 40 years.

"As announced by my predecessor, on 18 May 2011, we have approved initial gate investment in respect of the replacement programme and selected a submarine design". It was also confirmed that a study is being conducted to examine alternative systems and postures in accordance with the provision in the coalition agreement.

TYPE 26 FRIGATE (GLOBAL COMBAT SHIP)

The Type 26 Global Combat Ship project entered its Assessment Phase in March 2010, and a four-year contract was placed with BAE Systems Surface Ships to work with the MoD to produce a full design specification to be taken into the demonstration and build phases. This is the first class of vessel to emerge from the Sustained Surface Combatant

Capability (S2C2) programme - a 12-month study that yielded a bold plan to recapitalise the bulk of the sub-capital ship fleet through to 2035. The outcome of the study was to rationalise eight existing classes of warship down to just three. The capability currently delivered by the Type 22s and Type 23s would be replaced by C1, a Force Anti-Submarine Warfare and Land Attack Combatant and C2, a Stabilisation Combatant, while C3, an Ocean-Capable Patrol Vessel, would replace the RN's dedicated mine coun-termeasures (MCM) hulls but also offer additional capability for hydrographic and mar-itime security tasks. The Strategic Defence and Security Review, announced in October 2010 indicated that as soon as possible after 2020 the Type 23 would be replaced by the Type 26, designed to be easily adapted to change roles and capabilities depending on the strategic circumstances. However, the Type 26 will now embrace both the C1 and C2 requirements in one hull - estimated be be around 5,000 tonnes. The rebranding of the vessel as a Global Combat Ship is seen as an effort to make this class an attractive export proposition, and overseas participation in the programme has been sought.

From the outset cost has been a driving factor and the new ships will rely on a lot of technology already installed in the Type 45 and the Future Carrier programmes. For example, the new ARTISAN 3D Medium Range Radar being procured for the Type 23 capability upgrade will be transferred to the Type 26; the existing Sonar 2087 low frequency active/passive variable depth sonar will similarly migrate; the combat management system will be evolved from that of the current Outfit DNA(2)/CMS-1 combat system core; and the Future Local Area Air Defence System (Maritime), based on the new Common Anti-air Modular Missile, will be fitted first to Type 23, then to Type 26. A medium-calibre gun will be fitted. With an earlier BAE Systems 155mm option now withdrawn from consideration, the choice will be between the legacy Mk 8 Mod 1 4.5-inch (114mm) gun, and off-the-shelf 5-inch (127 mm) systems from BAE Systems and Oto Melara (the GCS design will be able to incorporate any gun currently on the market between 76 mm and 127mm).

What sort of precision land attack capability might be fitted remains the subject of further analysis (options include loitering munitions and long-range deep strike mis-siles). However, the ambition remains for Type 26 to be outfitted from build with strike length vertical launcher modules, thereby offering the flexibility to take a wide mix of suitably qualified weapons.

MILITARY AFLOAT REACH AND SUSTAINABILITY (MARS)

The future re-equipment of the RFA rests with this programme in which it is envisioned 11 ships will be procured (Five fleet tankers - delivered 2011 to 2015; Three joint sea-based logistics vessels - 2016, 2017 and 2020; Two fleet solid-support ships - 2017 and 2020 and a single fleet tanker - 2021).

At the end of 2007 the MoD invited industry to express their interest in the project to build up to six fleet tankers. In May 2008 four companies had been shortlisted to submit proposals for the design and construction of the ships - Fincantieri (Italy); Hyundai (Republic of Korea); Navantia (Spain) and BAE Systems, teamed with BMT DSL and DSME (Republic of Korea). Initially none of the bidders were to build the ships in the UK, however, in November 2008 Fincantieri had teamed up with Northwestern Shiprepairers and Shipbuilders (NSL) and if selected, two of the tankers could, potentially, be built at Birkenhead. However, this project was deferred in December 2008, the MoD announcing that having reviewed all the components of the MARS fleet auxiliary programme it was concluded that there was scope for considering alternative approaches to its procurement. Since that time it appears that the whole project has stalled, however a notice issued on 6 October 2009 by the Defence Equipment and Support (DE&S) organisation's Afloat Support (AfSup) directorate seemed to breathe new life into the programme as it launched a prequalification phase for interested industry parties, and, at the same time, revealed that it had broadened the scope of possible solutions. Post SDSR the government stated that the requirement for the MARS programme is driven by the logistic support needs of the future RN; these are being assessed following the outcome of the Strategic Defence and Security Review.

On the positive side an international competition was underway in 2011 for the MARS Tanker and the MoD hopes to announce the winning bidder early this year. The aspect of the MARS programme which aims to deliver the two solid stores ships remains uncommitted at this stage. The MoD stated that it is too early to provide any details of how this capability is to be taken forward, and the requirement is being assessed against the scope and duration of future planned operations.

THE ROYAL FLEET AUXILIARY

The Royal Fleet Auxiliary (RFA) is a civilian manned fleet, owned by the Ministry of Defence. Traditionally, its main task has been to replenish warships of the Royal Navy at sea with fuel, food, stores and ammunition to extend their operations away from base support. However, as the RN surface fleet has shrunk, the RFA has shrunk with it and a 'Value for Money' (VfM) review is being conducted to determine how best the support provided by the RFA can be delivered to the fleet.

The Strategic Defence and Security Review announced in October 2010 has further reduced the size of the RN and, as a consequence, the size of the RFA. One of the four Bay class LSD(A)s was to be withdrawn from service as was a Leaf class tanker and a Fort class AOR. It is believed that as part of the VfM review the RFA has to show 10% savings over the next 12 months.

Legislation banning the use of single-hulled tankers in 2010 is driving the need for replacement ships. There are three such dedicated tankers in-service with the RFA with a further general replenishment ship that has a tanking capability. However, such is the delay in the new tanker programme that the two Rover class tankers have had their service lives extended by a further seven years - making them 42 years old before they are expected to finally pay off.

As part of the Military Afloat Reach and Sustainability (MARS) programme, the MoD are to procure up to six new double-hulled Fleet Tankers, intended to replace the dedicated tankers and, along with the two existing Wave class ships, meet the RN's future tanking requirements, removing the need to utilise the general replenishment ship for tanking purposes. Final bids have been requested from the bidders in the ongoing international competition for the MARS Tanker contract. The MoD hope to announce the winning bidder early this year.

The long term maintenance of the RFA fleet rests with shipyards in the North West, North East and South West of England. Northwestern Shiprepairers and Shipbuilders (NSL) of Birkenhead and the A&P Group in Falmouth and Newcastle-upon-Tyne were named as the contractors to maintain the flotilla of 16 RFA tankers, stores and landing ships. They maintain 'clusters' of ships, providing the necessary refuelling and refit work for the RFA vessels throughout their service lives. Ships are grouped in clusters according to their duties and capabilities. A&P Group are charged with two clusters (Cluster 1: ARGUS and Cluster 2: CARDIGAN BAY, LYME BAY, MOUNTS BAY) in a contract worth around £53 million with the work to be shared between its bases in Falmouth and on the Tyne, while NSL is contracted for the maintenance of four clusters of ships (Cluster 3: ORANGELEAF, BLACK ROVER, GOLD ROVER; Cluster 4: DILIGENCE, WAVE KNIGHT, WAVE RULER; Cluster 5: FORT AUSTIN, FORT ROSALIE and Cluster 6: FORT VICTORIA), with contracts totalling over £180 million. The programme is expected to save over £330 million on the previous arrangements which saw individual contracts competed for as and when they were required.

SHIPS OF THE ROYAL FLEET AUXILIARY
Pennant Numbers

Ship	Pennant Number	Page	Ship	Pennant Number	Page
Tankers			**Amphibious Ships**		
ORANGELEAF	A110	45	LYME BAY	L3007	49
GOLD ROVER	A271	46	MOUNTS BAY	L3008	49
BLACK ROVER	A273	46	CARDIGAN BAY	L3009	49
WAVE KNIGHT	A389	44			
WAVE RULER	A390	44	**Repair Ship**		
Stores Ships			DILIGENCE	A132	50
FORT ROSALIE	A385	47	**Primary Casualty Receiving**		
FORT AUSTIN	A386	47	**Ship/Aviation Training Ship**		
Stores Ship/Oilers			ARGUS	A135	51
FORT VICTORIA	A387	48			

RFA Wave Ruler

FAST FLEET TANKERS
WAVE CLASS

Ship	Pennant Number	Completion Date	Builder
WAVE KNIGHT	A 389	2002	BAE SYSTEMS
WAVE RULER	A 390	2002	BAE SYSTEMS

Displacement 31,500 tons (Full Load) **Dimensions** 196 x 27 x 10m **Speed** 18 knots **Armament** 2 x Vulcan Phalanx (fitted for but not with), 2 x 30mm **Aircraft** Up to 2 Merlin **Complement** 80 (plus 22 Fleet Air Arm)

Notes

These 31,500-tonne ships are diesel-electric powered, with three refueling rigs. They have a cargo capacity of 16,900 tonnes (Fuel) and 915 tonnes (Dry Stores). They have a large one spot flight deck, hangar and maintenance facilities capable of supporting two Merlin helicopters. They have spent extended periods in the Caribbean conducting successful counter-narcotics operations with an embarked RN helicopter.

RFA Orangeleaf

SUPPORT TANKERS

LEAF CLASS

Ship	Pennant Number	Completion Date	Builder
ORANGELEAF	A110	1982	Cammell Laird

Displacement 37,747 tons **Dimensions** 170m x 26m x 12m **Speed** 14.5 knots
Complement 60

Notes

A single-hulled ex-merchant ship, originally acquired for employment mainly on freighting duties. A commercial Stat32 class tanker modified to enable it to refuel warships at sea. In 2007 she completed a Service Life Extension Programme (SLEP) refit which will enable her planned decommissioning in 2015.

The MoD also has the commercial tanker MAERSK RAPIER under charter. She is a multi-tasked tanker which supplies fuel to the naval facilities in the UK and abroad. The MoD charters the vessel to commercial companies when it is not in use for their own requirements.

RFA Black Rover

SMALL FLEET TANKERS
ROVER CLASS

Ship	Pennant Number	Completion Date	Builder
GOLD ROVER	A271	1974	Swan Hunter
BLACK ROVER	A273	1974	Swan Hunter

Displacement 11,522 tons **Dimensions** 141m x 19m x 7m **Speed** 18 knots **Armament** 2 - 20mm guns **Complement** 49/54

Notes

Small Fleet Tankers designed to supply warships with fresh water, dry cargo and refrigerated provisions, as well as a range of fuels and lubricants. Helicopter deck, but no hangar. Have been employed in recent years mainly as support for HM Ships operating around the Falkland Islands and as the FOST station tanker. Now 38 years old, GOLD ROVER was scheduled to decommission in 2009 and BLACK ROVER in 2010, but delays to the MARS programme have moved these dates back to 2016 and 2017 respectively.

46

RFA Fort Rosalie

STORES VESSELS
FORT CLASS I

Ship	Pennant Number	Completion Date	Builder
FORT ROSALIE	A385	1978	Scott Lithgow
FORT AUSTIN	A386	1979	Scott Lithgow

Displacement 23,384 tons **Dimensions** 183m x 24m x 9m **Speed** 20 knots
Complement 201, (120 RFA, 36 MoD Civilians & 45 Fleet Air Arm)

Notes

Full hangar and maintenance facilities are provided and up to four Sea King or Lynx helicopters can be carried for both the transfer of stores and anti-submarine protection of a group of ships (note: these ships are not cleared to operate Merlin). Both ships can be armed with 4 - 20mm guns. FORT AUSTIN began a regeneration refit in 2011 having been laid up at Portsmouth since 2009. It was planned to decommission FORT ROSALIE in 2013 and FORT AUSTIN in 2014, but in March 2011 it was announced that these dates had been revised to 2022 and 2021 respectively.

RFA Fort Victoria

REPLENISHMENT SHIPS
FORT CLASS II

Ship	Pennant Number	Completion Date	Builder
FORT VICTORIA	A387	1992	Harland & Wolff

Displacement 35,500 tons **Dimensions** 204m x 30m x 9m **Speed** 20 knots **Armament** 4 - 30mm guns, 2 x Phalanx CIWS, Sea Wolf Missile System (Fitted for but not with) **Complement** 100 (RFA), 24 MoD Civilians, 32 RN and up to 122 Fleet Air Arm

Notes

A "One stop" replenishment ship with the widest range of armaments, fuel and spares carried. Can operate up to 5 Sea King/Lynx or 3 Merlin Helicopters (more in a ferry role) with full maintenance facilities onboard. Medical facilities were upgraded with a 12 bed surgical capability. Under current plans she is to remain in service until 2019. A sister ship, FORT GEORGE, was withdrawn from service in 2011 as part of the SDSR. She is laid up at Liverpool awaiting disposal.

RFA Cardigan Bay (with Phalanx)

LANDING SHIP DOCK (AUXILIARY)
BAY CLASS

Ship	Pennant Number	Completion Date	Builder
LYME BAY	L3007	2007	Swan Hunter
MOUNTS BAY	L3008	2006	BAe SYSTEMS
CARDIGAN BAY	L3009	2007	BAe SYSTEMS

Displacement 16,190 tonnes **Dimensions** 176.6m x 26.4m x 5.1m **Speed** 18 knots
Armament Fitted to receive in emergency **Complement** 60

Notes

The dock is capable of operating LCU 10s and they carry two LCVP Mk5s. They can offload at sea, over the horizon. In addition to their war fighting role they could be well suited to disaster relief and other humanitarian missions. MOUNTS BAY emerged from refit at the end of 2010. She now has two funnels running up the side of the midships gantry. These were resited due to problems with fumes over the aft end of the flightdeck. Additional mini-gun emplacements have been added at the stern (in place of the aft funnels) and amidships. It is unknown at this time whether this is a trial fit or if the rest of the class will receive the same level of refit. CARDIGAN BAY is fitted with two Phalanx CIWS mounts. As a result of the SDSR LARGS BAY was withdrawn from service and transferred to the Royal Australian Navy where she was renamed HMAS CHOULES.

RFA Diligence

FORWARD REPAIR SHIP

Ship	Pennant Number	Completion Date	Builder
DILIGENCE	A132	1981	Oesundsvarvet

Displacement 10,595 tons **Dimensions** 120m x 12m x 3m **Speed** 15 knots **Armament** 2 - 20mm **Complement** RFA 40, RN Personnel - approx 100

Notes

Formerly the M/V STENA INSPECTOR purchased (£25m) for service in the South Atlantic. Her deep diving complex was removed. She is fitted with a wide range of workshops for hull and machinery repairs, as well as facilities for supplying electricity, water, fuel, air, steam, cranes and stores to other ships and submarines. When not employed on battle repair duties she can serve as a support vessel for MCMVs and submarines on deployment.

• DANIEL FERRO **RFA Argus**

PRIMARY CASUALTY RECEIVING
SHIP/AVIATION TRAINING SHIP

Ship	Pennant Number	Completion Date	Builder
ARGUS	A135	1981	Cantieri Navali Breda

Displacement 28,481 tons (full load) **Dimensions** 175m x 30m x 8m **Speed** 18 knots
Armament 4 - 30 mm, 2 - 20 mm **Complement** 254 (inc 137 Fleet Air Arm)
Aircraft 6 Sea King/Merlin.

Notes

The former M/V CONTENDER BEZANT was purchased in 1984 and rebuilt at Harland and Wolff, Belfast, from 1984-87 to operate as an Aviation Training Ship. She undertook a rapid conversion in October 1990 to a Primary Casualty Receiving Ship (PCRS) for service in the Gulf. These facilities were upgraded and made permanent during 2001. In 2009 the ship underwent a Service Life Extension Programme at Falmouth to switch her primary role to that of PCRS with a secondary aviation training role. The conversion has reduced helicopter capability by one landing spot and increased the efficiency of the primary care facility. Work undertaken included the construction of new casualty access lifts together with a new deckhouse aft of the superstructure; upgrade and structural modification to the bridge front; accommodation upgrades to cabins, galley & crew area; removal of starboard side vehicle ramp and installation of four additional watertight bulkheads. It has facilities for undertaking 3 major operations simultaneously, intensive care, high dependency and general wards for up to 100 patients. It also has a dentistry operating theatre, CT scanner and X-ray units. The care facility operates with a staff of up to 250 doctors, nurses and support staff. The ship is scheduled to remain in service until 2020.

MV Anvil Point

STRATEGIC SEALIFT RO-RO VESSELS
POINT CLASS

Ship	Pennant Number	Completion Date	Builder
HURST POINT		2002	Flensburger
HARTLAND POINT		2002	Harland & Wolff
EDDYSTONE		2002	Flensburger
LONGSTONE		2003	Flensburger
ANVIL POINT		2003	Harland & Wolff
BEACHY HEAD		2003	Flensburger

Displacement 10,000 tonnes, 13,300 tonnes (FL) **Dimensions** 193m x 26m x 6.6m
Speed 18 knots **Complement** 38

Notes

Foreland Shipping Limited (formerly AWSR) operates 6 ro-ro vessels built at yards in the UK and Germany under a PFI deal which was signed with the MoD on 27 June 2002 and runs until 31 December 2024. While the current main focus is on transporting equipment to and from the Middle East/Gulf in support of military activities in Afghanistan, the vessels also make regular voyages to the Falkland Islands and to Canada and Norway in support of training exercises. The six ships are all named after English lighthouses. The ships come under the operational umbrella of Defence Supply Chain Operation and Movements (DSCOM), part of the Defence Logistics Organisation.

HMS OCEAN

HMS DEFENDER

John Crae

Steve Wright

HMS SUTHERLAND

F81

HM Ships BLYTH and ATHERSTONE

John Newth

HMS TYNE

HMS PROTECTOR

Michael Barclay

A173

SERCO MARINE SERVICES

In December 2007 the MoD signed a £1 billion Private Finance Initiative (PFI) contract with Serco Denholm Marine Services Limited for the future provision of marine services (FPMS) over the next 15 years. In 2009 Serco bought out Denholm's share and the SD funnel logos are progressively being replaced by a prominent Serco logo on the superstructure.

Serco manage, operate and maintain around 110 vessels used in both port and deep water operations. As part of the new contract Serco is currently introducing 29 new vessels. The majority of these vessels have been constructed by the Netherlands based Damen Shipyards Group. Included are tugs, pilot boats and service craft. Most have been selected from Damen's standard product range and fitted out to the Serco's specification. Two classes of tug, the ASD Tug 2009 and the ATD 2909, have been purpose built as has the LMLBa 4315 SD OCEANSPRAY which operates with four different liquid cargoes.

Marine services embrace a wide range of waterborne and associated support activities, both in and out of port, at Portsmouth, Devonport and on the Clyde, as well as maintenance of UK and overseas moorings and navigational marks and support of a range of military operations and training.

In-port services include the provision of berthing and towage activities within the three naval bases; passenger transportation, including pilot transfers and the transportation of stores, including liquids and munitions. The recovery and disposal of waste from ships and spillage prevention and clean-up also fall within their tasking. There is also a requirement for substantial out-of-port operations. Diving training, minelaying exercises, torpedo recovery, boarding training and target towing duties are also undertaken.

The Briggs Group has been sub-contracted to assist with buoys and mooring support work. Shore based work to support these moorings and navigation buoys, have been relocated from Pembroke Dock to Burntisland on the Firth of Forth.

Initially all vessels were repainted with red funnels and hulls are now completely black, the white line having been removed as have, in most cases, the pennant numbers. All names are now prefixed with the letters 'SD' and all vessels fly the red ensign. New build vessels are being delivered without red funnels and it appears that the red funnels may disappear.

SHIPS OF
SERCO MARINE SERVICES

SD Impulse

TUGS

IMPULSE CLASS

Ship	Completion Date	Builder
SD IMPULSE	1993	R. Dunston
SD IMPETUS	1993	R. Dunston

G.R.T. 400 tons approx **Dimensions** 33m x 10m x 4m **Speed** 12 knots **Complement** 5

Notes

Completed in 1993 specifically to serve as berthing tugs for the Trident Class submarines at Faslane. To be retained in service until 2022.

SD Indulgent

ASD 2509 CLASS

Ship	Completion Date	Builder
SD INDEPENDENT	2009	Damen, Gorinchem
SD INDULGENT	2009	Damen, Gorinchem

G.R.T. 345 tons approx **Dimensions** 26.09m x 9.44m x 4.3m **Speed** 13 knots **Complement** Accommodation for 6. (12 passengers plus 3 crew max)

Notes

Azimuth Stern Drive (ASD) tugs based at Portsmouth. SD INDEPENDENT delivered 16 October 2009 and SD INDULGENT in January 2010. Designed for Coastal and Harbour towage, specifically modified for making cold moves within the Naval Bases. Both are based at Portsmouth.

SD Resourceful

ATD 2909 CLASS

Ship	Completion Date	Builder
SD RELIABLE	2009	Damen, Stellendam
SD BOUNTIFUL	2010	Damen, Stellendam
SD RESOURCEFUL	2010	Damen, Stellendam
SD DEPENDABLE	2010	Damen, Stellendam

G.R.T. 271 tons **Dimensions** 29.14m x 9.98m x 4.8m **Speed** 13.1 knots **Complement** 3 (Accommodation for 6)

Notes

Azimuthing Tractor Drive (ATD) tugs SD RELIABLE and SD BOUNTIFUL are based at Portsmouth. SD RESOURCEFUL and SD DEPENDABLE are based on the Clyde. Designed for Coastal and Harbour towage, specifically modified for making cold moves within the Naval Bases. Two double drum towing winches are fitted, along with extensive underwater fendering, fire fighting equipment and facilities for passenger and stores transportation.

SD Careful

TWIN UNIT TRACTOR TUGS (TUTT's)

Ship	Completion Date	Builder
SD ADEPT	1980	R. Dunston
SD CAREFUL	1982	R. Dunston
SD FAITHFUL	1985	R. Dunston
SD FORCEFUL	1985	R. Dunston
SD POWERFUL	1985	R. Dunston

G.R.T. 384 tons **Dimensions** 38.8m x 9.42m x 4m **Speed** 12 knots **Complement** 9

Notes

The principal harbour tugs in naval service. Some are to undergo a service life extension programme. SD POWERFUL moved to Devonport as an extra asset for use on Vanguard class submarine moves and to back fill any refit downtime for existing vessels. CAPABLE removed from service in 2011 and put up for sale at Gibraltar.

SD Hercules (with Towed Array Handling Equipment)

STAN TUG 2608 CLASS

Ship	Completion Date	Builder
SD HERCULES	2009	Damen, Gorinchem
SD JUPITER	2009	Damen, Gorinchem
SD MARS	2009	Damen, Gorinchem

G.R.T. 133.92 tons **Dimensions** 26.61m x 8.44m x 4.05m **Speed** 12 knots **Complement** 4 (6 max)

Notes

A conventional Twin Screw Tug design. SD HERCULES is based at Devonport. SD MARS and SD JUPITER are based on the Clyde. All can be used to handle submarine mounted Towed Arrays.

SD Christina

ASD 2009 CLASS

Ship	Completion Date	Builder
SD CHRISTINA	2010	Damen, Gdynia
SD DEBORAH	2010	Damen, Gdynia
SD EILEEN	2010	Damen, Gdynia
SD SUZANNE	2010	Damen, Gdynia

G.R.T. 120.74 tons **Dimensions** 21.2m x 9.4m x 3.6m **Speed** 11 knots **Complement** 5

Notes

Azimuth Stern Drive tugs derived from the successful Damen ASD 2411 shiphandling tug. Winches fore and aft, together with a bow thruster, make these tugs suitable for handling smaller surface ship, barge work and assisting with submarine movements. SD EILEEN and SD CHRISTINA are based at Devonport, SD SUZANNE and SD DEBORAH at Portsmouth. They are to replace SD FLORENCE, SD FRANCES, SD GENEVIEVE and SD HELEN.

SD Frances

FELICITY CLASS

Ship	Completion Date	Builder
SD FLORENCE	1980	R. Dunston
SD FRANCES	1980	R. Dunston
SD GENEVIEVE	1980	R. Dunston
SD HELEN	1974	R. Dunston

G.R.T. 88.96 tons **Dimensions** 22.0m x 6.4m x 2.6m **Speed** 10 knots **Complement** 4

Notes

Water Tractors used for the movement of small barges and equipment. Two sister vessels (GEORGINA and GWENDOLINE) sold to Serco Denholm in 1996 for service in H M Naval bases. To eventually be replaced by ASD 2009 class.

SD Emily

PUSHY CAT 1204

Ship	Completion Date	Builder
SD CATHERINE	2008	Damen, Gorinchem
SD EMILY	2008	Damen, Gorinchem

G.R.T. 29.4 tons **Dimensions** 12.3m x 4.13m x 1.55m **Speed** 8 knots **Complement** 3

Notes

Powered by a single Caterpillar 3056 TA diesel driving a single screw. A propulsion nozzle is fitted, and twin rudders to give a 2.1 tons bollard pull. SD CATHERINE is based at Portsmouth, SD EMILY at Devonport. General line runner and harbour work-boat.

SD Tilly

STAN TUG 1405

Ship	Completion Date	Builder
SD TILLY	2009	Damen, Gorinchem

G.R.T. 45 tons **Dimensions** 14.55m x 4.98m x 1.8m **Speed** 9 knots **Complement** 3

Notes

A general purpose inshore and harbour tug based at Devonport. A twin screw version of the Pushy Cat 1204. Slightly larger with a bow thruster and also developing 8 tonnes bollard pull. Line handler, general workboat and ideal for moving small barges.

SD Victoria

WORLDWIDE SUPPORT VESSEL

Ship	Completion Date	Builder
SD VICTORIA	2010	Damen, Galatz

G.R.T. 3,522 tons **Dimensions** 83m x 16m x 4.5m **Speed** 14 knots **Complement** 16 (Accommodation for 72)

Notes

Powered by two Caterpillar 3516B diesels driving two shafts with controllable pitch propellers SD VICTORIA is designed to support training operations around the world. Capable of transporting both personnel and equipment and supporting diving operations. She is equipped with classrooms, briefing rooms and operations rooms in addition to workshop facilities. There is provision to carry and operate RIBs and there is a helicopter winching deck.

SD Warden

TRIALS VESSEL

Ship	Completion Date	Builder
SD WARDEN	1989	Richards

Displacement 626 tons **Dimensions** 48m x 10m x 4m **Speed** 15 knots
Complement 11

Notes

Built as a Range Maintenance Vessel but now based at Kyle of Lochalsh and operated in support of BUTEC. Also operates as a Remotely Operated Vehicle (ROV) platform. A replacement ROV has been installed and set to work to replace the older system. To remain in service until 2022.

SD Kyle of Lochalsh

TRIALS VESSEL

Ship	Completion Date	Builder
SD KYLE OF LOCHALSH	1997	Abel, Bristol

Displacement 120 tons **Dimensions** 24.35m x 9m x 3.45m **Speed** 10.5 knots **Complement** 4

Notes

The former twin screw tug MCS LENIE which has now been purchased from Maritime Craft Services (Clyde) Ltd by Serco Marine Services. The 24.35m tug, built in 1997 by Abel in Bristol, is powered by Caterpillar main engines producing a total of 2,200bhp for a bollard pull of 26 tons. She is used to support trials and operations at Kyle.

A further trials craft, SARA MAATJE V, is on long term charter from Van Stee of Holland to assist with various tasks at the Kyle of Lochalsh facility.

SD Bovisand

TENDERS
STORM CLASS

Ship	Completion Date	Builder
SD BOVISAND	1997	FBM (Cowes)
SD CAWSAND	1997	FBM (Cowes)

G.R.T 225 tonnes **Dimensions** 23m x 11m x 2m **Speed** 15 knots **Complement** 5

Notes

These craft are used in support of Flag Officer Sea Training (FOST) at Plymouth to transfer staff quickly and comfortably to and from Warships and Auxiliaries within and beyond the Plymouth breakwater in open sea conditions. These are the first vessels of a small waterplane area twin hull (SWATH) design to be ordered by the Ministry of Defence and cost £6.5 million each. Speed restrictions implemented due to wash problems generated by these vessels. To remain in service until 2022.

SD Newhaven

NEWHAVEN CLASS

Ship	Completion Date	Builder
SD NEWHAVEN	2000	Aluminium SB
SD NUTBOURNE	2000	Aluminium SB
SD NETLEY	2001	Aluminium SB

Tonnage 77 tonnes (45 grt) **Dimensions** 18.3m x 6.8m x 1.88m **Speed** 10 knots
Complement 3 Crew (60 passengers)

Notes

MCA Class IV Passenger Vessels acquired as replacements for Fleet tenders. Employed
on general passenger duties within the port area. To remain in service until 2022. SD
NETLEY and NUTBOURNE are based at Portsmouth, NEWHAVEN at Devonport.

SD Padstow

PADSTOW CLASS

Ship	Completion Date	Builder
SD PADSTOW	2000	Aluminium SB

Tonnage 77 tonnes (45 grt) **Dimensions** 18.3m x 6.8m x 1.88m **Speed** 10 knots **Complement** 3 Crew (60 passengers)

Notes

MCA Class IV, VI and VIA Passenger Vessel based at Plymouth. Used on liberty runs in Plymouth Sound and the Harbour as well as occasionally supporting FOST. To remain in service until 2022.

SD Oban

OBAN CLASS

Ship	Completion Date	Builder
SD OBAN	2000	McTay
SD ORONSAY	2000	McTay
SD OMAGH	2000	McTay

G.R.T 199 tons **Dimensions** 27.7m x 7.30m x 3.75m **Speed** 10 knots **Complement** 5 Crew (60 passengers)

Notes

MCA Class IIA Passenger Vessels which replaced Fleet tenders in 2001. SD OBAN was transferred to Devonport in 2003 and is now primarily used to support FOST. SD ORONSAY and SD OMAGH employed on general passenger duties on the Clyde and are additionally classified as Cargo Ship VIII(A). To remain in service until 2022.

SD Norton

PERSONNEL FERRY

Ship	Completion Date	Builder
SD NORTON	1989	FBM Marine

G.R.T 21 tons **Dimensions** 15.8m x 5.5m x 1.5m **Speed** 13 knots **Complement** 2

Notes

The single FBM catamaran, 8837, operated at Portsmouth. Can carry 30 passengers or 2 tons of stores. Was a prototype catamaran designed to replace older Harbour Launches but no more were ordered.

SD Eva

PERSONNEL FERRY

Ship	Completion Date	Builder
SD EVA	2009	Damen

G.R.T 168 tons **Dimensions** 33.21m x 7.4m x 3.3m **Speed** 23.4 knots **Complement** 4-6 (plus 34 passengers)

Notes

Operated on the Clyde as a Fast Crew Transport. With an Axe Bow design she has replaced SD ADAMANT. The Axe Bow design allows the vessel to effectively cut through waves with minimal movement of the vessel. The vessel is the first of its type in the UK to be operated under the International Code of Safety for High Speed Craft (HSC Code).

SD Menai

FLEET TENDERS

Ship	Completion Date	Builder
SD MELTON	1981	Richard Dunston
SD MENAI	1981	Richard Dunston
SD MEON	1982	Richard Dunston

G.R.T. 117.3 tons **Dimensions** 24m x 6.7m x 3.05m **Speed** 10.5 knots **Complement** 4/5 (12 passengers)

Notes

The last three survivors of a once numerous class of vessels used as Training Tenders, Passenger Ferries, or Cargo Vessels. MENAI and MEON are operated at Falmouth. MELTON is operated at Kyle. A vessel replacement programme now seems unlikely and this elderly trio are expected to remain in service until 2022.

SD Teesdale

COASTAL OILER

Ship	Completion Date	Builder
SD TEESDALE	1976	Yorkshire Drydock Co.

G.R.T. 499 tons **Dimensions** 43.86m x 9.5m x 3.92m **Speed** 8 knots **Complement** 5

Notes

Formerly the oil products tanker TEESDALE H operated by John H Whitaker. Operates as a parcel tanker delivering diesel and aviation fuel and also delivering / receiving compensating water. She is self propelled by two Aquamaster thrusters.

A Diesel Lighter Barge, SD OILMAN, was delivered to the Clyde in late November 2009 and a Water Lighter Barge, SD WATERPRESS, was delivered in November 2010, also for operation on the Clyde. A further barge, a Liquid Mixed Lighter Barge, SD OCEANSPRAY, was delivered in June 2010 and is based at Portsmouth. The elderly tanker SD OILPRESS and the water tanker SD WATERMAN are to be withdrawn from service.

SD Tornado

TORPEDO RECOVERY VESSELS (TRV) TORNADO CLASS

Ship	Completion Date	Builder
SD TORNADO	1979	Hall Russell

G.R.T. 560 tons **Dimensions** 47.1m x 9.15m x 3m **Speed** 14 knots **Complement** 12

Notes

She has had suitable rails fitted to enable her to operate as an exercise minelayer. Converted in 2002 to support RN diving training (in lieu of Fleet Tenders) in addition to her other roles. Operates on the Clyde. SD TORMENTOR was put up for sale in 2010.

SD Salmoor

MOORING & SALVAGE VESSELS
SAL CLASS

Ship	Completion Date	Builder
SD SALMOOR	1985	Hall Russell

G.R.T 1,967 tons **Dimensions** 77.1m x 14.92m x 4m **Speed** 15 knots **Complement** 12

Notes

Multi-purpose vessels designed to lay and maintain targets, navigation marks and moorings. Based at Greenock and can be deployed in support of submarine and sub-marine rescue operations. SD SALMAID decommissioned in 2011.

SD Moorfowl

MOOR CLASS

Ship	Completion Date	Builder
SD MOORFOWL	1989	McTay Marine
SD MOORHEN	1989	McTay Marine

Displacement 518 tons **Dimensions** 32m x 11m x 2m **Speed** 8 knots **Complement** 10

Notes

Designed as a powered mooring lighter for use within sheltered coastal waters. SD MOORHEN has since been converted and now day runs as a diving /support tender from Kyle in support of BUTEC and for diver training courses. The lifting horns have been removed from the bows of both vessels. To remain in service until 2022.

SD Navigator

MULTICAT 2510 CLASS

Ship	Completion Date	Builder
SD NAVIGATOR	2009	Damen, Hardinxveld
SD RAASAY	2010	Damen, Hardinxveld

G.R.T 150.27 tons **Dimensions** 26.3m x 10.64m x 2.55m **Speed** 8 knots
Complement Accommodation for 6 (plus 9 passengers)

Notes

SD NAVIGATOR is equipped for buoy handling with a single 9 ton capacity crane. She is capable of supporting diving operations. SD RAASAY was delivered on 1 January 2010 and based at the Kyle of Lochalsh. She is fitted with two cranes for torpedo recovery and support diving training. SD NAVIGATOR is managed from Devonport, but operates between Devonport and Portsmouth. Two similar vessels, SD INSPECTOR (ex-DMS EAGLE) and SD ENGINEER operate from Portsmouth and Devonport respectively.

SD Tamar Racer

STAN TENDER 1505 CLASS

Ship	Completion Date	Builder
SD CLYDE RACER	2008	Damen, Gorinchem
SD SOLENT RACER	2008	Damen, Gorinchem
SD TAMAR RACER	2008	Damen, Gorinchem

Displacement 100 tons **Dimensions** 16m x 4.85m x 1.25m **Speed** 20 knots **Complement** 3 (+ 10 Passengers)

Notes

Of aluminium construction these boats are employed on transfer of pilots, port security operations and passenger and VIP transportation. CLYDE RACER delivered 20 June 2008; SOLENT RACER 19 September 2008 and TAMAR RACER 10 December 2008.

SD Solent Spirit

STAN TENDER 1905 CLASS

Ship	Completion Date	Builder
SD CLYDE SPIRIT	2008	Damen, Gorinchem
SD SOLENT SPIRIT	2008	Damen, Gorinchem
SD TAMAR SPIRIT	2008	Damen, Gorinchem

Displacement 100 tons **Dimensions** 18.91m x 5.06m x 1.65m **Speed** 21.7 knots **Complement** 3 (+ 10 passengers)

Notes

Steel hull with aluminium superstructure. Special propeller tunnels are fitted to increase propulsion efficiency and to reduce vibration and noise levels. These vessels are able to operate safely and keep good performance in wind speeds up to Force 6 and wave heights of 2 metres. Employed on transfer of pilots, VIPs and personnel. SD CLYDE SPIRIT delivered 27 June 2008; SD SOLENT SPIRIT 25 July 2008 and SD TAMAR SPIRIT delivered on 17 October 2008.

Kingdom of Fife

ANCHOR HANDLING TUG

Ship	Completion Date	Builder
KINGDOM OF FIFE	2008	Damen, Galatz

Displacement 1,459 tons **Dimensions** 61.2m x 13.5m x 4.75m **Speed** 13.7 knots **Complement** 18

Notes

Briggs Marine won a £100m contract from Serco to support navigation buoy mainte-nance and mooring support for the Royal Navy for the next 15 years. During the con-tract period, Briggs Marine provide support for over 350 moorings, navigation buoys and targets for the RN all around the UK coast, as well as Cyprus, Gibraltar and the Falkland Islands. KINGDOM OF FIFE was delivered in May 2008 and supports the existing Briggs Marine shallow draught and heavy lift craft CAMERON in servicing the contract, and is equipped with a decompression chamber and its own dedicated dive support team.

Smit Don

AIRCREW TRAINING VESSELS

Ship	Comp Date	Builder	Base Port
SMIT DEE	2003	BES Rosyth	Buckie
SMIT DART	2003	BES Rosyth	Plymouth
SMIT DON	2003	BES Rosyth	Blyth
SMIT YARE	2003	FBMA Cebu	Great Yarmouth
SMIT TOWY	2003	FBMA Cebu	Pembroke Dock
SMIT SPEY	2003	FBMA Cebu	Plymouth

G.R.T. 95.86 GRT **Dimensions** 27.6m x 6.6m x 1.5m **Speed** 21 knots **Complement** 6

Notes

The service for Marine Support to Ranges and Aircrew Training is provided by SMIT (Scotland) Ltd and runs until April 2017. These vessels provide for training military aircrew in marine survival techniques, helicopter winching drills, target towing and general marine support tasks. More recently they have participated in Navy Command boarding exercises, simulating arms and drug smuggling activities and force protection exercises involving both Fast Attack Craft and Fast Inshore Attack Craft. SMIT DART completed as a passenger vessel with a larger superstructure. Two similar, second-hand vessels, SMIT TAMAR and SMIT CYMRYAN, are also employed in a similar role.

Smit Rother

RANGE SAFETY VESSELS

Ship	Comp Date	Builder
SMIT STOUR	2003	Maritime Partners Norway
SMIT ROTHER	2003	Maritime Partners Norway
SMIT ROMNEY	2003	Maritime Partners Norway
SMIT CERNE	2003	Maritime Partners Norway
SMIT FROME	2003	Maritime Partners Norway
SMIT MERRION	2003	Maritime Partners Norway
SMIT PENALLY	2003	Maritime Partners Norway
SMIT WEY	2003	Maritime Partners Norway
SMIT NEYLAND	2003	Maritime Partners Norway

G.R.T. 7.0 tons **Dimensions** 12.3m x 2.83m x 0.89m **Speed** 35 knots **Complement** 2

Notes

A class of 12 metre Fast Patrol Craft which operate on Range Safety Duties at Dover, Portland and Pembroke. Have replaced the former RCT Sir and Honours class launches in this role.

RCTV Aachen

RAMPED CRAFT LOGISTIC

Vessel	Pennant Number	Completion Date	Builder
ARROMANCHES	L105	1987	James & Stone
ANDALSNES	L107	1984	James & Stone
AACHEN	L110	1986	James & Stone
AREZZO	L111	1986	James & Stone
AUDEMER	L113	1987	James & Stone

Displacement 290 tonnes (Laden) **Dimensions** 33.3m x 8.3m x 1.5m **Speed** 10 knots
Complement 6.

Notes

Operated by the Army's 17 Port and Maritime Regiment, Royal Logistic Corps, these all purpose landing craft are capable of carrying up to 96 tons. They are self sustaining for around five days or a thousand nautical miles before requiring replenishment either at sea or in a haven. In service in UK coastal waters. ANDALSNES is operated by 417 Maritime Troop at Cyprus. ARROMANCHES was formerly AGHEILA (re-named 1994 when original vessel was sold). Most vessels sport a green and black camouflage scheme.

AIRCRAFT OF THE FLEET AIR ARM

MIKE BATTEN

AgustaWestland MERLIN HM1, HM2

Role Anti-submarine and Maritime surveillance
Engine 3 x Rolls-Royce Turbomeca RTM322 turboshafts each developing 2,100 shp
Length 74' 10" **Width** 14' 10" **Height** 21' 10" **Main Rotor Diameter** 61'
Max Weight 32,120 lbs
Max Speed 167 kts **Range** 625 nm
Crew 3 – each crew position has a tactical display so an extra pilot, observer or air-crewman can be carried in the co-pilot position for specific missions.
Avionics Blue Kestrel 360 degree radar; Orange Reaper ESM; Folding Light Acoustic System for Helicopters (FLASH); AQS 903A acoustic processor; defence aids including directional infrared counter-measures (DIRCM), AN/AAR-57 missile approach warning system, chaff and flare dispensers; Wescam MX-15 electro-optical/IR camera fitted to a number of deployed aircraft.
Armament 1 x M3M 0.5" gun in cabin door; 1 x GPMG in cabin window; up to 4 Stingray torpedoes; up to 4 Mark 10 depth charges.
Squadron Service 814, 820, 824, 829 Naval Air Squadrons

Notes

All 4 development aircraft and the first production-standard Merlin HM2 were flying by the end of 2011. The first 2 production aircraft are to complete release-to-service trials at RNAS Culdrose in August 2012; trials aircraft operate from Boscombe Down. Full-scale production began in January 2012 and is due to complete in December 2014 with up to 10 aircraft on the 'pulse line' at any one time and a 'new' aircraft delivered to the RN every six weeks. Work on each aircraft takes eight months. HM2s will be allocated to squadrons from 2013 with initial operational capability following in 2014. 814 and 820 NAS each have 6 aircraft at present and 11 crews, each of which comprises a pilot, observer and sensor operator. 829 NAS provides flights for Type 23 frigates; each of which has two-pilot crews to increase flexibility. All are base-ported at RNAS Culdrose when not embarked, together with 824 NAS, the training unit

CROWN COPYRIGHT/MoD

AgustaWestland MERLIN HC3, HC4

Role Anti-submarine and Maritime surveillance
Engine 3 x Rolls-Royce Turbomeca RTM322 turboshafts each developing 2,100 shp
Length 74' 10" **Width** 14' 10" **Height** 21' 10" **Main Rotor Diameter** 61'
Max Weight 32,120 lbs
Max Speed 167 kts **Range** 625 nm
Crew 3 – each crew position has a tactical display so an extra pilot, observer or aircrewman can be carried in the co-pilot position for specific missions.
Avionics Blue Kestrel 360 degree radar; Orange Reaper ESM; Folding Light Acoustic System for Helicopters (FLASH); AQS 903A acoustic processor; defence aids including directional infrared counter-measures (DIRCM), AN/AAR-57 missile approach warning system, chaff and flare dispensers; Wescam MX-15 electro-optical/IR camera fitted to a number of deployed aircraft.
Armament 1 x M3M 0.5" gun in cabin door; 1 x GPMG in cabin window; up to 4 Stingray torpedoes; up to 4 Mark 10 depth charges.
Squadron Service 814, 820, 824, 829 Naval Air Squadrons

Notes

During 2012 preparations to transfer Merlin battlefield support helicopters from the RAF to the RN Commando Helicopter Force will gather momentum with an initial 12 aircrew and 35 maintenance engineers converting to operate the type. The aircraft themselves will undergo a Life Sustainment Programme, drawing wherever possible on experience with work on the HM2 and making the aircraft as closely compatible with it as possible, using common training and logistic support management. In RN service the aircraft will be designated Merlin HC4 and will be modified with the same 'glass' cockpit and power-folding main rotor-head as the HM2 and a new folding tail pylon. The type has a rear-loading ramp which allows light vehicles, artillery and bulk loads to be carried internally. The limited original RAF specification for the HC3 prevented it from operating at sea and the sustainment programme will include the installation of flotation gear, lashing points and telebrief equipment. The Merlin HC4 will be able to carry 24 marines in crash-resistant seating or a disposable lift of up to 8,800lb. It will be based at RNAS Yeovilton.

AgustaWestland SEA KING

Sea Kings are to be withdrawn from service by 2016. By then the type will have been in service with the RN for forty-seven years and earned the respect of generations of air-crew and maintenance engineers. The different versions will be replaced in different ways by different types.

Engines 2 x 1600shp Rolls Royce Gnome H 1400 – 1 free power turbines.
Length 54' 9" **Height** 17' 2" **Max Weight** 21,400lb **Rotor Diameter** 62' 0"
Max Speed 125 knots (HC 4+ 145 knots).

NICK NEWNS

HAR 5

Roles Utility; COD (Carrier Onboard Delivery); SAR, aircrew training
Crew 2 pilots, 1 observer and 1 aircrewman/winchman.
Avionics Sea Searcher radar; Star Safire III EO/IR camera turret.
Armament A 7.62mm machine gun can be mounted in the doorway if required.
Squadron Service 771 Naval Air Squadron

Notes

771 NAS provides SAR coverage in the south-west from RNAS Culdrose. The unit also provides type training for ASaC and utility Sea King aircrew and maintainers. A detach-ment of 3 aircraft operate from Prestwick Airport, covering a vast area of Scotland,

Northern Ireland and 200 miles beyond Ireland into the Atlantic. By 2016 the Government expects the UK SAR mission to be carried out by contracted civilian helicopters, some of which may be flown by naval pilots. The HAR5 is to be withdrawn from service when this new system comes into operation but it is not yet clear whether 771 NAS will be retained for a utility role with another type or be de-activated'

• LEE HOWARD

ASaC 7

Role Airborne Surveillance and Control of both maritime and land operations.
Crew 1 pilot and 2 observers.
Avionics Cerberus mission-system; Searchwater radar; Orange Crop ESM; Joint Tactical Information Distribution System (Link 16). AN/AAR-57 missile approach warning system; IR jammer, radar-warning receiver; auto chaff and flare dispenser.
Squadron Service 849, 854, 857 Naval Air Squadrons.

Notes

854 and 857 NAS maintain a continuous detachment in Afghanistan with each unit deployed for a year during which personnel are rotated. They provide wide area surveillance of even the smallest moving objects over land, passing information to land-based coalition forces by data-link. The deployed aircraft have 'Carson' rotor blades, a five-bladed tail-rotor and enhanced engines which give a 30% increase in performance in 'hot and high' conditions. Two aircraft from 849 NAS spent part of 2011 embarked in HMS OCEAN as part of the RN contribution to NATO operations over Libya. All three squadrons are based at RNAS Culdrose where 849 fulfils a training as well as a contin-

gency operational role. Although the Cerberus mission system is 'state-of-the-art', the ASaC7 airframes are among the oldest in RN service and are due to be replaced in 2016 by a new maritime surveillance and control aircraft (MASC). The 'funding assumption' for this is a version of the Merlin fitted with Cerberus, either some or all of the 12 not brought up to HM2 standard or some of the 30 HM2s made capable of 'swinging' between ASaC or sea control missions with podded Cerberus equipment. Another option is the procurement of E-2 Hawkeye aircraft with training given by the USN and logistic support shared with the French Navy.

• MIKE BATTEN

HC 4

Role Commando assault, load-lifting and tactical helicopter operations.
Crew 1 or 2 pilots and 1 aircrewman. About 25% of the aircrew are Royal Marines.
Armament 1 x M3M 0.5" gun in cargo door and 1 x 0.762mm GPMG in crew-entry door to give 360 degree sweeping fire when needed
Squadron Service 845, 846 and 848 Naval Air Squadrons.

Notes

The detachment of HC4s maintained in Afghanistan since 2007 formally ended in September 2011. Operational availability in the Commando Helicopter Force (CHF) is likely to be reduced over the next few years as aircrew and engineers are trained to operate Merlins but the Sea King will not finally be replaced until 2016. The CHF is based at RNAS Yeovilton and comprises 845 and 846 NAS, 848 NAS which combines operational capability with a training role, 847 NAS and a Headquarters Squadron. They are capable of operation afloat or ashore in any climate, anywhere in the world'

• MIKE BATTEN

AgustaWestland LYNX

Variants HMA 8 (SRU), AH 9A.

Roles Surface search and strike; anti-submarine strike; boarding party support; light reconnaissance and troop carrying.

Engines 2 x Rolls-Royce Gem BS 360-07-26 free power turbines each developing 900 shp.

Length 39' 1" **Height** 11' 0" **Max Weight** 9,500lb **Rotor diameter** 42' 0" .

Max Speed 150 knots. **Crew** 1 pilot and 1 observer.

Avionics : Sea Spray radar; Orange Crop ESM; Sea Owl Electro-Optical/Infrared camera (HMA 8); Second-generation Anti-jam Tactical UHF Radio for NATO (SATURN) including Successor IFF and Digital Signal processor in HMA 8 (SRU). **Armament** External pylons for up to 4 Sea Skua ASM or 2 Stingray torpedoes. 1 door mounted M3M 0.5" gun and 1 hand-held Heckler & Koch G 3 sniper rifle to provide Precision Anti-Personnel Sniping (PAPS) in support of boarding parties in case they are opposed.

Squadron Service 702, 815 and 847 Naval Air Squadrons.

Notes

The HAS3 variant was withdrawn from operational service in 2011 but a few examples remain in use temporarily for training purposes ashore. 815 NAS provides operational flights to a variety of warships and RFAs; Type 45 class destroyers embark 2 Lynx, most other ships one. 702 NAS is a training unit which has an operational capability and 847 NAS operates the AH7 as a light strike and reconnaissance unit within the CHF. All are based at RNAS Yeovilton. The last Lynx will be withdrawn at the end of 2015 when the replacement Wildcat becomes operational.

AgustaWestland WILDCAT

Variants HMA 1.
Roles Maritime Search and Strike; Boarding Party Support.
Engines: 2 x LHTEC CTS 800 turboshafts each rated at 1362shp
Length 50' 0" **Height** 12' 0" **Max Weight** 13,200lb **Rotor diameter** 42' 0"
Max Speed 157 knots   **Crew** 1 pilot and 1 observer.
Avionics Selex-Galileo Sea Spray 7400E multi-mode Active Electronically Scanned Array, AESA, radar; Wescam MX-15 EO/IR camera. Defensive aids suite.
Armament Future air-to-surface guided weapon in both light and heavy versions; Stingray torpedoes; Mark 11 depth-charges; door mounted M3M 0.5" gun.
Squadron Service 700W Naval Air Squadron.

Notes

Trials with both Naval and Army versions of the Wildcat are proceeding well and ship compatibility trials are due to take place in RFA ARGUS during 2012. The first of the 28 production aircraft on order for the RN will be delivered in 2012 and a release-to-service is expected in 2013. The first naval Wildcats will begin operational evaluation in 2014 with initial operational capability in early 2015. Under present plans both RN and Army versions of the type are, initially, to be based at RNAS Yeovilton and 700W is manned as a joint unit.

TAILORED AIR GROUPS

ILLUSTRIOUS, OCEAN and big-deck RFAs operate Tailored Air Groups (TAG) comprising helicopters embarked for specific operations. They can also operate allied helicopters when necessary alongside British types. For example, during NATO operations against Libyan forces in 2011 OCEAN operated Army Apache AH1 attack helicopters; RN Sea King ASaC7 surveillance and control helicopters and US Black Hawk long-range combat SAR helicopters in case it proved necessary to recover downed aircrew from deep inside enemy territory. ILLUSTRIOUS is capable of embarking USMC, Spanish, Italian or even Thai Harriers but her ship's company would need time to work up before they could be operated efficiently.

FIXED WING OPERATIONS

SDSR 2010 left the RN with no fixed-wing fighter squadrons in commission but the knowledge of how to operate them at sea must be kept alive to generate squadrons of F-35C Lightning IIs for QUEEN ELIZABETH and PRINCE OF WALES. This is being achieved by close co-operation with the US Navy which is allowing up to six RN pilots to train in the USA and fly F/A-18s from US carrier decks at any one time. The UK has 3 F-35Bs on order, legacies of earlier interest in the STOVL type, one of which may be exchanged for an F-35C if current negotiations succeed, and these will enable RN pilots to participate in operational development work in the USA. When the UK orders its first production batch of F-35Cs, deliveries are likely to follow after about five years with operational capability of the first unit some two years later. If an order is placed in 2012, therefore, the first RN F-35C unit might become operational in 2019.

AgustaWestland APACHE

Variants AH 1
Role Attack and reconnaissance helicopter.
Engines 2 x Rolls Royce/Turbomeca RTM 322 turboshafts.
Length 58' 3" **Height** 15' 3" **Max Weight** 15,075lb **Rotor Diameter** 17' 2"
Max Speed 150 knots **Crew:** 2 pilots
Avionics Helicopter Integrated Defensive Aids Suite (HIDAS); Longbow radar, optical and infra-red target acquisition sensors.
Armament Up to 16 AGM 114 Hellfire anti-tank guided weapons; up to 4 Sidewinder air-to-air missiles; M230 30mm cannon with 1,160 rounds (chain gun); up to 76 CRV 7 unguided rockets.
Operator Operated by the Army Air Corps as part of the Joint Helicopter Force.

Notes
Apaches operated from OCEAN with success in 2011 as one of the elements of the UK contribution to operations over Libya. They are likely to be embarked more frequently in future but attention must be paid to limiting the impact of corrosion caused by operating in the salt-laden environment over the sea.

Boeing CHINOOK

Variants HC 2
Role Battlefield transport helicopter.
Engines 2 x 3,750 shp Avco Lycoming T55-L-712 turboshafts.
Length 98' 9" **Height** 18' 8" **Max Weight** 50,000lb **Rotor Diameter** 60' 0"
Max Speed 160 knots **Crew** 2 pilots, 1 aircrewman.
Avionics Infra-red jammer; chaff & flare dispenser, missile warning system.
Armament Up to 2 x M 134 miniguns and 1 x M 60 machine gun.
Operator Operated by the RAF as part of the Joint Helicopter Force.

Notes

The principal troop and load-lifting helicopter in the JHF, Chinooks can embark in ILLUS-TRIOUS and OCEAN for amphibious operations. They lack power-folding for their rotor blades and are too big to be struck down the lifts into the hangars of the current generation of carriers. Blades have to be removed to stow the aircraft into a deck park to free the deck for other helicopter operations. QUEEN ELIZABETH will be able to strike down Chinooks fully-spread on the side lifts into her large hangar and operate the type in significant numbers when necessary. A new batch of Chinooks is on order for the RAF.

OTHER AIRCRAFT TYPES IN ROYAL NAVY SERVICE DURING 2012

BAE Systems HAWK

Engine 1 x Adour Mk 151 5200 lbs thrust.
Crew 1 or 2 Pilots

Notes
Used by the Fleet Requirements and Aircraft Direction Unit (FRADU) at RNAS Culdrose to provide support for RN and foreign ships working-up with FOST; with the RN Flying Standards Flight and as airborne targets for the Aircraft Direction School. The aircraft are operated by Babcock and have civilian pilots and maintainers.

Eurocopter AS365N DAUPHIN 2

Engines 2 x Turbomeca Arriel 1C1.
Crew 1 or 2 pilots.

Notes

Operated by British International from Plymouth City Airport under a Civil-Owned Military Registered, COMR, contract with the MOD, these 2 helicopters are used to transfer FOST staff to ships in the Plymouth Areas, for guided-weapons system calibration and naval gunfire support training. Their future base is unknown as Plymouth airport was scheduled to close in 31 December 2011.

• CROWN COPYRIGHT/MoD 2011

Beech AVENGER T1

Engines 2 x Pratt & Whitney PT 6A turboprops.
Crew 1 or 2 pilots; up to 4 student observers plus instructors.

Notes

4 aircraft, known in RN service as the Avenger and developed from the King Air 350 ER, began operations with 750 NAS training observers in October 2011 replacing the Jetstream. Their introduction coincided with a new observer training syllabus in which the first two phases are flown in the Grob Tutors of 703 NAS at Barkston Heath and the third in Avengers at RNAS Culdrose.

LEE HOWARD

GROB TUTOR T1

Engine 1 x Lycoming 0 - 360 - A1B6 piston engine
Crew 1 or 2 pilots

Notes
Used by 703 NAS at RAF Barkston Heath for the elementary training of RN pilots and observers and by 727 NAS at RNAS Yeovilton for the flying grading of new entry aircrew and other light, fixed-wing tasks.

ADRIAN PINGSTONE

Eurocopter SQUIRREL HT1

Engine 1 x Turbomeca Ariel 1D1
Crew 1 or 2 pilots and up to 4 passengers

Notes
Used by 705 Squadron (numbered in the RN sequence but not commissioned as a Naval Air Squadron) at RAF Shawbury as part of the Defence Helicopter Flying School (DHFS) to provide initial helicopter training for RN pilots before they move on to Sea King, Merlin or Lynx training units at RN air stations.

Royal Navy Historic Flight

The Royal Navy Historic Flight, based at RNAS Yeovilton, consists of several historic aircraft kept on the military register, maintained by civilians under a MoD contract and flown by the unit's commanding officer assisted by volunteer naval pilots in the display season. The present collection includes Swordfish I W 5856, Swordfish II LS 326, Sea Fury FB 11 VR 930, Sea Fury T 20 VX 281, Sea Hawk WV 908 and Chipmunk T 10 WK 608. They are not usually all serviceable at the same time. Swordfish III NF 389 continues to undergo long-term restoration by BAE Systems at Brough.

Galileo MIRACH 100/5

Used by 792 NAS, the Fleet Target Group based at RNAS Culdrose to provide targets for missile shoots by the remaining Sea Dart equipped destroyers. Mirach can be launched from ships at sea and, if not destroyed, they parachute into the sea and can be refurbished for further use

WEAPONS OF THE ROYAL NAVY

Sea Launched Missiles

Trident II D5

The American built Lockheed Martin Trident 2 (D5) submarine launched strategic missiles are Britain's only nuclear weapons and form the UK contribution to the NATO strategic deterrent. 16 missiles, each capable of carrying up to 6 UK manufactured thermonuclear warheads (but currently limited to 4 under current government policy), can be carried aboard each of the Vanguard class SSBNs. Trident has a maximum range of 12,000 km and is powered by a three stage rocket motor. Launch weight is 60 tonnes, overall length and width are 13.4 metres and 2.1 metres respectively.

Tomahawk (BGM-109)

This is a land attack cruise missile with a range of 1600 km and can be launched from a variety of platforms including surface ships and submarines. Some 65 of the latter version were purchased from America to arm Trafalgar class SSNs with the first being delivered to the Royal Navy for trials during 1998. Tomahawk is fired in a disposal container from the submarine's conventional torpedo tubes and is then accelerated to its subsonic cruising speed by a booster rocket motor before a lightweight F-107 turbojet takes over for the cruise. Its extremely accurate guidance system means that small targets can be hit with precision at maximum range, as was dramatically illustrated in the Gulf War and Afghanistan. Total weight of the submarine version, including its launch capsule is 1816 kg, it carries a 450 kg warhead, length is 6.4 metres and wingspan (fully extended) 2.54 m. Fitted in Astute & T class submarines.

Harpoon

The Harpoon is a sophisticated anti-ship missile using a combination of inertial guidance and active radar homing to attack targets out to a range of 130 km, cruising at Mach 0.9 and carrying a 227 kg warhead. Fitted to Type 23 frigates. It is powered by a lightweight turbojet but is accelerated at launch by a booster rocket.

Sea Viper (Aster 15/30)

Two versions of the Aster missile will equip the Type 45 Destroyer, the shorter range Aster 15 and the longer range Aster 30. The missiles form the weapon component of the Principal Anti Air Missile System (PAAMS). Housed in a 48 cell Sylver Vertical Launch system, the missile mix can be loaded to match the ships requirement. Aster 15 has a range of 30 km while Aster 30 can achieve 100 km. The prime external difference between the two is the size of the booster rocket attached to the bottom of the missile. PAAMS is to be known as Sea Viper in RN service.

Sea Dart

A medium range area defence anti aircraft missile powered by a ramjet and solid fuel booster rocket. Maximum effective range is in the order of 80 km and the missile accelerates to a speed of Mach 3.5. It forms the main armament of the Type 42 destroyers. Missile weight 550 kg, length 4.4 m, wingspan 0.91 m.

Sea Wolf

Short range rapid reaction anti-missile missile and anti-aircraft weapon. The complete weapon system, including radars and fire control computers, is entirely automatic in operation. Type 23 frigates carry 32 Vertical Launch Seawolf (VLS) in a silo on the foredeck. Basic missile data: weight 82 kg, length 1.9 m, wingspan 56 cm, range c.5-6 km, warhead 13.4 kg. The VLS missile is basically similar but has jettisonable tandem boost rocket motors.

Air Launched Missiles

Sea Skua

A small anti-ship missile developed by British Aerospace arming the Lynx helicopters carried by various frigates and destroyers. The missile weighs 147 kg, has a length of 2.85 m and a span of 62 cm. Powered by solid fuel booster and sustainer rocket motors, it has a range of over 15 km at high subsonic speed. Sea Skua is particularly effective against patrol vessels and fast attack craft, as was demonstrated in both the Falklands and Gulf Wars.

Guns

114mm Vickers Mk8

The Royal Navy's standard medium calibre general purpose gun which arms the later Type 22s, Type 23 frigates and Type 42 destroyers. A new electrically operated version, the Mod 1, recognised by its angular turret, was introduced in 2001 and will be fitted in the Type 23, Type 42 and Type 45 classes. Rate of fire: 25 rounds/min. Range: 22,000 m. Weight of Shell: 21 kg.

Goalkeeper

A highly effective automatic Close in Weapons System (CIWS) designed to shoot down missiles and aircraft which have evaded the outer layers of a ships defences. The complete system, designed and built in Holland, is on an autonomous mounting and includes radars, fire control computers and a 7-barrel 30 mm Gatling gun firing 4200 rounds/min. Goalkeeper is designed to engage targets between 350 and 1500 metres away.

Phalanx

A US built CIWS designed around the Vulcan 20 mm rotary cannon. Rate of fire is 3000 rounds/min and effective range is c.1500 m. Fitted in Destroyers, OCEAN, Wave, Bay and Fort Victoria classes. Block 1B began entering service from 2009. Incorporates side mounted Forward looking infra-red enabling CIWS to engage low aircraft and surface craft.

DS30B 30mm

Single 30mm mounting carrying an Oerlikon 30mm gun. Fitted to Type 23 frigates and various patrol vessels and MCMVs. In August 2005 it was announced that the DS30B fitted in Type 23 frigates was to be upgraded to DS30M Mk 2 to include new direct-drive digital servos and the replacement of the earlier Oerlikon KCB cannon with the ATK Mk 44 Bushmaster II 30 mm gun. Consideration is already being given to purchasing additional DS30M Mk 2 systems for minor war vessels and auxiliaries.

GAM BO 20mm

A simple hand operated mounting carrying a single Oerlikon KAA 200 automatic cannon firing 1000 rounds/min. Maximum range is 2000 m. Carried by most of the fleet's major warships except the Type 23 frigates.

20mm Mk.7A

The design of this simple but reliable weapon dates back to World War II but it still provides a useful increase in firepower, particularly for auxiliary vessels and RFAs. Rate of fire 500-800 rounds/min.

Close Range Weapons

In addition to the major weapons systems, all RN ships carry a variety of smaller calibre weapons to provide protection against emerging terrorist threats in port and on the high seas such as small fast suicide craft. In addition it is sometimes preferable, during policing or stop and search operations to have a smaller calibre weapon available. Depending upon the operational environment ships may be seen armed with varying numbers of pedestal mounted General Purpose Machine Guns (GPMG). Another addition to the close in weapons is the Mk 44 Mini Gun a total of 150 of which have been procured from the United States as a fleetwide fit. Fitted to a naval post mount, the Minigun is able to fire up to 3,000 rounds per minute, and is fully self-contained (operating off battery power).

Torpedoes

Stingray

A lightweight anti submarine torpedo which can be launched from ships, helicopters or aircraft. In effect it is an undersea guided missile with a range of 11 km at 45 knots or 7.5 km at 60 knots. Length 2.1 m, diameter 330 mm. Type 23s have the Magazine Torpedo Launch System (MTLS) with internal launch tubes. Sting Ray Mod 1 is intended to prosecute the same threats as the original Sting Ray but with an enhanced capability against small conventionally powered submarines and an improved shallow-water performance.

Spearfish

Spearfish is a submarine-launched heavyweight torpedo which has replaced Tigerfish. Claimed by the manufacturers to be the world's fastest torpedo, capable of over 70 kts, its sophisticated guidance system includes an onboard acoustic processing suite and tactical computer backed up by a command and control wire link to the parent submarine. Over 20ft in length and weighing nearly two tons, Spearfish is fired from the standard 21-inch submarine torpedo tube and utilises an advanced bi-propellant gas turbine engine for higher performance.

Future Weapons

Future Anti-Surface Guided Weapon (Heavy)

This project, led by MBDA (UK) and derived from the company's existing 15km range Sea Skua Anti-Ship Missile, will provide the lead in to a 100kg weapon family that will include the Selected Precision Effects at Range (SPEAR) air-launched weapon for the Royal Air Force. Using an Imaging Infra Red (IIR) seeker capability, the project will be developed in collaboration with France, which has a similar anti-ship missile requirement, the Anti Navire Léger. It will provide the main armament for the RN's AW159 Lynx Wildcat and the French Navy's NH90 and Panther helicopters.

Future Anti-Surface Guided Weapon (Light)

Led by Thales (UK), this project will be based on the company's 6-8km range Lightweight Multi-role Missile (LMM). Weighing just 13kg it is designed to be fired from multiple ground, air and naval platforms against an equally wide range of targets up to, but not including Main Battle Tanks (MBTs). The RN variant is being developed to operate from the AW159 Lynx Wildcat helicopter.

Future Local Area Air Defence System – Maritime (FLAADS-M)

Incorporating the Common Anti-Air Modular Missile (CAAMM) family, being developed to replace the Rapier and Seawolf SAM systems, plus the ASRAAM short range Air-to-Air Missile, this project will be led by MBDA (UK). FLAADS-M will arm the Royal Navy's Type 23 frigates and its Type 26 Global Combat Ships.

At the end of the line ...

Readers may well find other warships afloat which are not mentioned in this book. The majority have fulfilled a long and useful life and are now relegated to non-seagoing duties. The following list gives details of their current duties:

Pennant No	Ship	Remarks
	BRITANNIA	Ex Royal Yacht at Leith. Open to the public.
	CAROLINE	Light Cruiser and veteran of the Battle of Jutland. Remains at Belfast. Future uncertain.
M29	BRECON	Hunt Class Minehunter - Attached to the New Entry Training Establishment, HMS RALEIGH, Torpoint, as a static Seamanship Training ship.
M103	CROMER	Single Role Minehunter - Attached to Britannia Royal Naval College, Dartmouth as a Static Training ship.
L3505	SIR TRISTRAM	Refitted as a Static Range Vessel at Portland.
C35	BELFAST	World War II Cruiser Museum ship - Pool of London. Open to the public daily. Tel: 020 7940 6300
D23	BRISTOL	Type 82 Destroyer - Sea Cadet Training Ship at Portsmouth.
D73 S17	CAVALIER OCELOT	World War II Destroyer & Oberon class Submarine Museum Ships at Chatham. Open to the public. Tel: 01634 823800
F126 M1115	PLYMOUTH BRONINGTON	The ships remain at Birkenhead whilst discussions over their future continue.
S21	ONYX	At Barrow awaiting a new future as a proposed Submarine Heritage Centre will not now be opened.
S67	ALLIANCE	Submarine - Museum Ship at Gosport Open to the public daily. Tel: 023 92 511349
S50	COURAGEOUS	Nuclear-powered Submarine - On display at Devonport Naval Base. Can be visited during Base Tours. Visit Royal Navy website or Tel: 01752 553941 for details.

Pennant No	Ship	Remarks
M1151	IVESTON	Static Sea Cadet Training Vessel (Thurrock)

At the time of publishing (December 2011) the following ships were laid up in long term storage or awaiting sale.

PORTSMOUTH: Ark Royal; Gloucester; Manchester; Chatham; Campbeltown; Walney; Bayleaf.

PLYMOUTH: Cornwall; Cumberland; Trafalgar; Sceptre; Superb; Splendid; Spartan; Sovereign; Conqueror; Valiant; Warspite.

ROSYTH: Resolution; Renown; Repulse; Revenge; Swiftsure; Churchill; Dreadnought.

LIVERPOOL: Fort George.

Since the previous edition the following vessels in long term storage or awaiting scrap were disposed of:

INVINCIBLE Left Portsmouth on 24 March 2011, in tow of tug SCIROCCO, to be scrapped at Leyal Ship Recycling in Alaiga, Turkey.

EXETER Left Portsmouth on 22 September 2011, in tow of Netherlands-Antilles registered tug COMPASS, to be scrapped at Leyal Ship Recycling in Aliaga, Turkey.

NOTTINGHAM Left Portsmouth on 19 October 2011, in tow of Maltese registered tug SPARTAN, to be scrapped at Leyal Ship Recycling in Aliaga, Turkey.

SOUTHAMPTON Left Portsmouth on 14 October 2011, in tow of tug PANTODYNAMOS, to be scrapped at Leyal Ship Recycling in Aliaga, Turkey.

LARGS BAY In April 2011 it was announced that the ship had been bought by the Royal Australian Navy for £65 million. Following a UK refit the ship was handed over to the RAN on 14 October and renamed HMAS CHOULES.